CONTROL MINDSET

CONTROL MINDSET

AN INTERACTIVE GUIDE TO
FREEING YOUR MIND,
TAKING CONTROL, AND UNLOCKING
THE EXTRAORDINARY

NICOLETTE KHALIFIAN

NEW DEGREE PRESS

CONTROL MINDSET

An interactive guide to freeing your mind, taking control, and unlocking the extraordinary

ISBN   978-1-64137-408-8   *Paperback*

            978-1-64137-409-5   *Kindle Ebook*

            978-1-64137-410-1   *Digital Ebook*

CONTENTS

WHY I AM WRITING
THIS BOOK

———

Why am I sitting here collecting a stretch of thoughts as I question each and every one, contemplating if it is worthy enough to be shared in print, questioning if what I envision for myself, for others, and for global communities is even relevant? Why am I doing this?

I am doing this because there is no valid reason not to. I could easily give up my power to the voices of those around me, to the people who don't believe in me, to all the stress I can convince myself will follow a book launch. I can psych myself out of it quite easily; we all can. But upon realizing the power of now, the power of saying YES, I have been freed. I have been unleashed into a life of freedom, peace, and complete control. I am manifesting that freedom and writing a book. I am taking a leap. I am finally freeing myself from the strings I had been tied to my entire life. It all starts with the mind. It all starts from within.

The power to write and share, the power to be vulnerable and authentic, is a power I have never understood or valued until I saw the wonders it did for others.... I discovered the power to tell stories, to empathize, and to *help* others are *not* limited to age. I discovered each and every one of us has a story to tell or knowledge to share that cannot be kept inside due to the fear or worry *they are not good enough*. No one should be restricted from freeing themselves, from unleashing themselves into a life of freedom and peace, merely because of some number with which we all identify.

By listening, by pushing ourselves to be genuinely interested in other people, we allow ourselves to *hear* what someone has to say, and we learn more than we ever thought possible. Forming a genuine interest and allowing that interest to spark conversation, interaction, and ultimately a sharing of knowledge is one of the most powerful abilities humans have. We must take advantage of this ability.

> *We are all teachers. We are all students.*
> *Form a burning desire to learn and to teach.*

We must form **a genuine interest** in the stories others have to share, as this is the pivotal learning point for each and every one of us. The moment I allowed myself to listen more carefully, the moment I *paid closer attention*, was the moment I learned more about myself than I ever thought possible.

Instill a burning desire to listen, **a burning desire to learn. We are all teachers just as we are all students.** So I ask you: bring the classroom to life.

You, the middle-schooler next door, and the professor at your local university, from the most accomplished to those who are just beginning their years of formal education. **Knowledge and experiences do not have a threshold for when they can be shared and when they are of value.** We all have a story to tell. There is no exception.

Take children: children have an understanding of life so coated by innocence that it is, in all of its entirety, what we should be chasing after ourselves.... Everyone has a lesson to share. Everyone is a teacher, with youth being some of the most valuable among us.

For example, what are toddlers like?.

They are fearless.
They are vulnerable.
They are authentic.

These are large claims to make. But if we dissect each of them, we will see how obvious they lie.

They are fearless. Toddlers *do not care to fail.* We all have footage of ourselves falling to the floor attempt after attempt when trying to learn how to walk. We looked foolish and adorable. A baby who was able to learn how to walk on their first attempt has never existed. Every fall is filled with laughter and claps which come from the family members watching.

The experience is joyous. Love fills the room. The failure of individuals who are *not* toddlers should likewise be treated as such! Why should we frown upon ourselves when falling down? Rather, it should be *instinctive*, just as it is for the toddler learning to walk, to pick ourselves back up and try to accomplish our goal.

They are vulnerable. Babies love to cry. Their emotions are worn on their sleeves. When they are happy, it is clear. When they are sad, it is clear. They express when they *need* something or someone. Their "baby pride" does not get in the way for it does not exist. They ask for help when they need it. They cry when they feel emotional. They laugh when they feel joyous. They share their feelings to those they trust. They are vulnerable. They do not limit themselves. They are free.

They are authentic. Babies aren't trying to be someone they're not. Are they? Have you ever called a baby fake or said they were trying to fit in? Do they care what other babies think? Absolutely not. They rock whatever outfit they were thrown into and take the town. They celebrate their uniqueness. They are authentic.

Yet as the years go on, we seem to lose sight of these incredible qualities which we all once had. Our job is to fight for them and get them back. These three qualities—the power to be fearless, vulnerable, and authentic—are what will give us the power to unleash into the most incredible life possible; only once fear is removed from the equation are we unstoppable.

I urge you to find value in the stories you have accumulated thus far in your life, for they are all *worthy* of *sharing! Remove fear from the equation and free yourself.*

For if we are able to judge, then we are able to formulate some type of thought.... We each hold different perspectives; this is utter proof that we each have something to say! What is stopping us from saying it? **What is stopping you from saying what you have to say? What are you afraid of?**

Every voice deserves to be heard—every story deserves to be shared. Our stories are only shared once we are no longer afraid of sharing them ... or once we are stuck with the realization we have nothing to lose ... But what if with every moment we live on this earth, we are never subject to loss unless we let ourselves be?

Not everyone is going to like what you are doing. Not everyone is going to appreciate your voice. Not everyone is going to listen. That is never going to change.... So why live as a prisoner to what you have no control over?

The limitations you believe exist are ones you have created for yourself and are not real. You have no limitations except the internal ones you create for yourself as a way to avoid what you actually want to accomplish. Release yourself from these constraints. **Let go.**

CHASE what lights you up, CHASE what you might be just a little curious about... Do not let the irrelevant, roaming thought of "I can't" have any power against you. I chased my vision of bringing *Control Mindset* to life, and here you are, reading it. Let go and run after what fuels you, whatever it may be.

Whether false understanding you have due to your age, your resources, your schedule, or what judgement you believe will follow, release yourself from those strings. Become fearless in your pursuit of *what you want to experience.* Celebrate your life—there is *no* guarantee more years are to come, that once you achieve X you can *finally* achieve Y. You can achieve Y *whenever you take the concrete steps to achieve Y.*

Pursuing your goals and becoming your vision is a celebration of your life. Taking control is a celebration of your life, for it is a power you are finally putting to use that you otherwise would let sit idly by. Celebrate your life. Value change. Be excited by fear. Become obsessed with failure. Become addicted to saying yes. **Grow allergic to excuses.**

Become addicted to saying yes.

X is a roadblock you are reluctant to accept, a roadblock you have created for yourself due to the excuses you keep reaching for out of the comfort they bring.

"I will finally be happy once I get that promotion."
"I will start going out once I lose the weight."
" I will start setting goals around the New Year."
"I will start working out once I have the time."
"I will focus on my friends once I'm not bombarded with work."
"I will focus on self-improvement once school is out."

Sound familiar? Excuses, ah, so comforting. They add a delay, they postpone the experiences we are so dearly afraid to experience.

Take the leap. Take control. WHAT IS STOPPING YOU FROM LIVING YOUR LIFE TO ITS FULLEST POTENTIAL? From living it in the most extraordinary sense possible?

Gary Vaynerchuk, entrepreneur, author, speaker, and internet personality, explains the **power of now** in one of his talks:

"When you see a ninety-year-old regret from not doing or living their lives by somebody else's point of view ... you will get so scared ... it will completely change the course of how you live your life. It stuns me in what we do due to the opinions of others."

— GARY VAYNERCHUK

It stuns me what we do due to the opinions of others.

Are the decisions you make solely because *you want to make those decisions? Do you truly have free will?*

Do you want to be a ninety-year-old sitting in regret?

If you answered no, do you believe you have the power to control your fate?

The third question is the only question in this book that has a correct answer. *The answer is yes.* You have the potential to live an extraordinary life. Excuses must vanish, fears must lose their power, your self-knowledge must be your greatest asset, and you must have a burning desire to experience the extraordinary. Only then will it be yours.

And so, I am dodging X and running after Y. I am here to tell my story.

I urge you to take control with me through the next few hundred pages. Take the leap. Overcome the internal limitations you have created for yourself. Strive for excellence in every way possible. This book was created so it could be referred back to time after time, to be personalized to the reader in every way possible. You deserve to live a life you are utterly obsessed with. Do not allow yourself to settle for the ordinary. Strive for better.

"Be in love with your life. Every minute of it."
—JACK KEROUAC

***

I began reading and writing every single day in order to exercise my writing muscles as much as I could. I brainstormed for days on end, questioning how I was going to combine everything I've learned and researched into a book that could speak to the masses. I let myself be the most vulnerable I had ever been. I fell into a life of self-inquiry and discovery. I began to listen more than I ever thought possible.

Everything that would otherwise just be a typical conversation was transformed into an experience that could spark an idea and writing of some sort. Everyone around me became a teacher. I was stunned by how much I could learn by merely paying closer attention … by listening just a little harder.

All of my energy went toward bringing what was once a foolish dream to life. Nothing was going to stop me except the ever-present thought that I was not good enough, an idea I worked tirelessly to crush. I am doing this because I refuse to patiently wait until the time is right to say what I have to say. *There is no timeline.* Living our lives by a strict timeline is like trying to live by a rulebook that doesn't exist. **It's all in your head.** *The time is now. Your time is now.* Why wait and follow what you believe is expected of you? Who are you trying to please? What are you trying to follow?

> *Living our lives by a strict timeline is like trying to live by a rule book that doesn't exist.*

I am following *my* rule book. I am following *my* timeline. I am sharing my voice. I am telling my story. I want you to do the same. Break the rules. Experience the extraordinary.

"Life is the most difficult exam. Many people fail because they try to copy others, not realizing that everyone has a different question on the paper."

—JEREMY MCGILVREY

As I share with you the lessons that have completely turned my life around, I urge you to believe in the value of *your* voice ... of *your* story.

No rubric or set of expectations must be followed in order for your story to be worthwhile. No set of standards must be met in order for your story to be relevant. Rather, it must gain some sort of audience, and whoever that audience may be, the story being shared should resonate with at least one member of the audience.

Simply, the story must have an effect, and that effect—whatever it might be—is as powerful as you let it be. I am sharing what has come from my internal struggles, crises, and countless self-revelations so at least one individual will resonate, feel heard, and be inspired enough to finally take the leap and change their life.

I hope my experiences, the lessons I have learned, and the perspective on life I have developed through my most dear lows are able to resonate with at least one reader. I hope my story connects with at least one of you.... For then I have succeeded.

I hope what I have spent the last nineteen years carefully crafting is able to connect with at least one of you in a way that helps you discover more about yourself than you ever thought possible and grow concretely with strength, resilience, and joy.

Thank you for taking this leap with me. Let's begin.

HOW TO GAIN CONTROL
WITH THIS BOOK

—

This book requires two things: a physical tool and a mental tool. The physical tool is a writing utensil of some sort. I hope you write all over every page, highlight, throw in question marks where you are confused and exclamation points where you feel an aura of enlightenment, when something *makes sense* and just *clicks*.

The mental tool is your *willingness* to seek *concrete change*. If you are not willing, if you are not open to varied perspectives and seeking new understandings, then this book will be of no value to you. Everything starts with the mind. Believe in your abilities. Believe in your potential. Believe in yourself. Be willing.

Accept your imperfections. Embrace your strengths. Believe in your ability to improve. Please, believe in yourself. Believe in the process. Believe in how much potential you have to be extraordinary, to live an extraordinary life. Come to terms with your weaknesses; don't let them push you away, but rather, have a stronger desire to chase after your vision and bring it to life. But more importantly, accept that you are deserving of bringing your vision to life in the first place.

The most important aspect of this book when working with my publisher was having the interactive element, the ability for readers to *act* on what they have just read about rather than merely reading. So, embedded throughout are writing prompts, quotes, fill-in-the-blanks, and tables that require your focus to write all over. But your time spent using your physical tool, whether it be a pencil, your favorite pen, or even a crayon will only be worthwhile if your *head is in the game.*

Let this book be your guide. Let my words, my stories, and the information I have gathered through countless days of research serve as inspiration and guidance for you, as a means to prompt self-discovery through an organic, solitary process.

Let this book make you think. Let this book make you question. Let this book make you question your *entire being.* Let it drive you crazy if need be. And then let it make you feel peace like you've never felt before. Let it guide you toward stability, your center.

Let this book spur disagreement. I don't expect anyone to agree with all of what I say. These are just my thoughts, my ideas, and my realizations formulated into text for me to share. I've seen these methods change lives just as they have changed mine. Counter what I say. Counter it all if you wish to.

GETTING IN CONTROL IS LIKE BUILDING A HOME.
It requires a set of materials, or building blocks, a construction phase where you follow an ultra-specific blueprint, and the maintenance that follows a newly built home. It does not happen overnight—control is a process that requires time and energy. However, once the process is completed, the end result is absolutely beautiful, and you will be unbelievably proud of what you have built.

1. The **building blocks** are the sets of practices that will help set up the foundation for your home. These building blocks apply to each and every home; they are not the details that are home-specific. These include generalized practices that *work*. They are the foundation. They prepare you to take on your blueprint. I will provide you with the building blocks. I will provide you with the tools. Your job is to figure out how you are going to use these tools and what other materials you need.

2. The **blueprint** is the most important part of the building process. The blueprint is ultra *user-specific*. The blueprint for every home is drastically different, because every home has different needs. Your home may have a pool where the one next door has a fountain; both require different blueprints to build. Here is where you concretely *take action*. The blueprint is specific to *you* and *your life*.

3. **Maintenance** is where you will check up on yourself and make changes accordingly. Once a home is built, there are always tweaks to be made. You may have painted the walls yellow but later decided you want to go for baby pink. Stay in touch with your vision and make changes accordingly. Nothing is permanent. Stay aligned through change.

The end of each chapter or subsection is followed by a template for your **control card.** Your control card is the most powerful aspect of this book, providing you with a space to build your home, to get in control. Your control card is only as powerful as you let it be; recite it every morning and every evening. Stay in tune with what you want to take control of. Become the vision you wish to bring to life. Your control card is your secret weapon. It is vital that you are specific in the wording of your control card and that you use words that resonate with *you*. The control card is *yours*. On the next page is a sample control card for reference.

GET IN CONTROL

INTENTION + ACTION = CONTROL = CHANGE

1. METHODS (YOUR BUILDING BLOCKS)
Here I will include a set of practices/
methods that are proven to work. These are
the foundation for your end result.

2. AFFIRMATIONS (YOUR BLUEPRINT)
Here is where you will get ultra-specific with your goals
and affirmations. Your blueprint must be so specific that
anyone can build what is on it. Writing in the present
tense creates instant accountability and manifestation.
You are making a promise to yourself. Your job is to keep
this promise, as the promises you make to yourself are the
most important.

*I take control and have regained my power from
fear. I work tirelessly and formed a burning desire to
no longer let my fear of failure stand in my way.*

3. CHECK INS & ADJUSTMENTS
(YOUR MAINTENANCE)
Here, write how you will check in with yourself. The
use of the present tense is again vital. You can rewrite
the paragraph below if it resonates strongly with you.

*I stay in tune with my vision by reciting my control card
every morning and every night. I check up on my goal
card in order to make changes as needed. As my environment changes, I adapt accordingly. I am a stable*

force, unbothered by the noise around me. I check up with what may be missing and make changes accordingly in order to return to my center and stay in control.

This book is YOURS.

I wanted to include this page as a sort of map for the direction *Control Mindset* will be taking. It may not make sense now, but as you read along, the pieces will begin to come together. The following are stages you will be guided through as the book progresses:

THE CONTROL MINDSET CENTRAL PHILOSOPHY MAP

ACCEPTANCE
UNDERSTANDING
SELF KNOWLEDGE
DESIRES
BURNING DESIRES
LIMITS
DEFEAT
MANIFESTATION
OPTIMIZATION
REMNANTS
THE FLOW STATE
PROTECTION OF THE FLOW STATE
DEVIATION FROM THE FLOW STATE
THE EXTRAORDINARY

INTRODUCTION

———

Every single one of us has two highly-specific things in common: Besides our body compositions, being part of the same species, and every other obvious thing humans share, we each have a beginning and an ending, varied, of course, in how they arise. We are all born into this life, and we all leave this life at some point in time. Simply, we're all going to die someday. At one point in time, we are going to be left with nothing. All of our pain, miseries, successes, moments of distress or utter euphoria, self-doubts, the thoughts that keep us up at night and distract us from what actually matters ... where will they go? Of the life we lived, what will remain from it? If we could choose, what exactly *would* we want to have lasted, to have made it through the seemingly barricaded death bed?

Most of us would probably prefer not to think about this question. Thinking about the limited time we are given and the best possible way to spend it brings great pressure. If we knew we only had X amount of minutes left, the decisions we would make, the people we would speak to and the aspirations we'd pick up would drastically change—timelines move people. **Deadlines move people.**[1] Life has a deadline. Each and every single one of us has a deadline. We must turn in the life we have created at some point—but the irking feeling of the unknown, the irking feeling of never being told when that deadline is **stops us from feeling the pressure that we need to feel.** We've convinced ourselves this deadline is imaginary, this deadline **doesn't exist.** Tomorrow will come and so will the day after that. Next month is just thirty days away and it will be here soon. We've convinced ourselves of this mindset to put ourselves at ease, because why bother to think about anything different? Why bother to think about everything just ending?

Because once we do—once we think about loss and how real it truly is—everything changes. We begin to sit in regret for what we should have done, for what we should have said or what we should have worked toward. In that very moment— the moment everything is taken away—we wish we could change something. We need to move our minds; we need to gain the mindset that rather makes us feel the pressure deadlines give—because only then will we move, only then will we understand what we deserve. Only then will we go after it.

The power of presence, the power of staying present and filling yourself with gratitude for every little thing you are experiencing at that very moment, helps achieve that goal.[2] It creates the pressure to appreciate everything around you,

1   Burnett, Dean. "The Power of Deadlines | Dean Burnett." *The Guardian*, April 20, 2015, sec. Science.

2   Hedges, Kristi. The Power of Presence: Unlock Your Potential to Influence and Engage Others. United States, AMACOM, 2017.

to appreciate what you are experiencing, and, in turn, to throw away what is distracting you from that exact feeling of presence and ease. And what could that feeling possibly be? But most importantly, what is stopping us from doing what we want to do? What is stopping us from experiencing what we deserve to experience, that once we have a deadline that feeling suddenly goes away? Fear.

The moment we are given a deadline, we go full-force into some project, goal, or aspiration. We suddenly become fearless. We suddenly forget all the hesitations that arise from the possibility of failing or that stem from discomfort.

I am going to tell you that today is your last day on this earth. Pretend that is the case. Close your eyes and envision how you would feel if you knew today was your last day. You already know you wouldn't think about certain things, and you would *definitely* think about countless other things. Those things that you would think about are clearly of high importance to you. Those that have been deemed irrelevant on this very day are probably not that important to you. Of those that are important to you, how do you handle them in your everyday life? Do you treat them with such importance? Are they as high priority as they are on your last day?

On your last day, likely priorities are important people, bucket-list thoughts, personal adventures that are meaningful to you, and some things you want to do because you just don't care anymore, because it's your *last shot*. Let's visit the last item: things you've always wanted to do but didn't. Your desire arises from knowing it is your last shot. Before, you were afraid. What does this indicate?

YOUR FEARS HAVE CONTROL OVER YOU—OUR FEARS HAVE CONTROL OVER US.[3]

We might not speak our minds because we are afraid those around us might not agree. We might not turn in a job application because we are afraid we are not qualified. We might not reach out to a friend who has become distant because we are afraid they don't care about us anymore. We don't experience most that we deserve to experience because we are **afraid.**

Once we accept this mere fact and live purposefully every single day to reclaim the power we have given these fears and instead use that power to empower ourselves to be fearless, **we are unstoppable.** We must become fearless without a deadline. We must become fearless in our everyday lives, for **only then can we reach the extraordinary.... Only then are we unstoppable.**

I used to be the *ideal* victim to fear. I was terribly afraid of nearly everything: the world, people. I was afraid of my thoughts. I was afraid of saying yes. I found deep comfort in saying no. I limited myself more than I ever thought possible without even realizing it.

I was afraid of what could go wrong. I was afraid of who I was and if this person would be accepted by others. I was so afraid of letting my light shine that, in time, I eventually lost it. I had no light to shine.

---

3   Intention Inspired. "How Fear Is Controlling Your Life," April 13, 2018.

I was afraid I was a constant bother. I was afraid I had no reason to be on this Earth. I was afraid I didn't belong here. I was afraid.

List five things you are not typically comfortable doing, five things that scare you. They can be anything. Sharing certain posts on social media, talking about certain subjects in conversation, standing up in a large room where everyone is seated ... anything. Just five. We will return to this later.

5 FEARS: LISTED

1

2

3

4

5

I lived fearing what could go wrong, what was not possible, what would happen if I took the leap, all the **failures** that would follow my attempts.

Fear—it's deadly. It's toxic. It ruins lives. Fear is cancerous, yet no one tries to find a cure. We live with it. We accept it. We are humans—the most brilliant species to ever live, yet we live, again, passively, with this absolute cancerous feeling. We are *okay* with being afraid, then proceed to fill ourselves with complaints and excuses as to why we can't accomplish something, why something didn't work out, why our past is written as it is, why our stories are told the way they are. How would your story change if you were **fearless**?

How would your story change if you were fearless?

But first, do you *know* what your greatest internal fears are? Do you know what is even stopping you in the first place?

I emphasize **internal fears** for these are the greatest form of a limiting fear—**they are obstacles we create for ourselves.**

I didn't say what I had to say because I was afraid I would be misunderstood.

I didn't ask my professor my burning question because I was afraid I was the only one who didn't understand what was being taught.

I didn't open up to my friend about how I felt hurt because I was afraid they would leave me.

I didn't reach out to a friend because I was afraid they didn't want to hang out with me.

I didn't speak up because I was afraid my thoughts weren't valid.

I didn't share something I was passionate about on Instagram because I was afraid it was irrelevant, that no one would care, that I would be judged in return.

I didn't like a post on Facebook because I was afraid of who would see.

I didn't make jokes because I was afraid no one would laugh.

I didn't initiate conversation because I was afraid of initiating conversation.

I didn't speak up because I thought I would be shut down.

I didn't share my interests because I felt no one would relate.

What's the pattern? I didn't do what I wanted to do, I didn't say what I wanted to say, because I was afraid of what would go wrong. I was afraid of failing.

And so I asked myself, what would I do if I wasn't afraid of failure? What would I do if it was *guaranteed* to just *work out?*

It was time for me to be fearless. It was time for me to start living.

Failure is our oxygen. We need it. We live off of it. Life doesn't exist without it. So why be afraid of it? Embrace it. Love it. Crave it. More in Part 1: Accept & Acknowledge.

"Our deepest fear is not that we are inadequate. Our deepest fear is that we are powerful beyond measure. It is our light, not our darkness that most frightens us. We ask ourselves, who am I to be brilliant, gorgeous, talented, fabulous? Actually, who are you not to be? ... And as we let our own light shine, we unconsciously give other people permission to do the same. As we are liberated from our own fear, our presence automatically liberates others."

—MARIANNE WILLIAMSON

"As we let our own light shine, we unconsciously give other people permission to do the same. As we are liberated from our own fear, our presence automatically liberates others."

I ask you to hold onto that quote, to dissect it and allow it to resonate with you as we dive deeper into fears in Part 1.

I was stuck in the could be, not the will be. This loop was driven by multiple factors of course, but the primary driving force—the driving force that threw me into every box possible and took more efforts than anything before to prop open—**control. I let my fears control my life. And so I was miserable, undeniably miserable.**

Engaging in a relationship with a friend that was clearly failing—a relationship that was an 80/20, where effort was clearly lopsided—was of course, not my fault, but rather the fault of the *universe.* My relationships suffered, no solution or concrete cause existed. I was simply left to experience a series of unfortunate events. That's what I convinced myself.

Dreading class because of how much I thought I loathed the material was expected and normalized. A privileged, public education was the last thing I was grateful for. I was used to losing sleep each night to thoughts that would venture into places I thought I had blocked off. I could see no end; I thought I would experience it forever. I had no control over the headspace I would fall into every night after ten. Tapping into a stream of solutions was simply *foolish* for there were none. I thought nothing would help me, so I didn't even bother trying.

Constant strain and arguments with my parents and siblings were normal; a regular conversation about anything—college, friends, life, my future, or goals would be a dream come true. A miracle.

My mind was stuck. My mind was consumed by my ability to convince myself change was foolish to dream of. Rock bottom was where I belonged. I deserved this. The world was out to get me, and I just had to deal with it. I had no control over my life. I'd been defeated.

Yet, the control unarguably existed, but I didn't know I had it. I felt the world had control over me, as if I was some puppet, obedient to every direction my life took and every decision made. I didn't believe I had that superpower, a superpower I desperately needed to start to use. I didn't know how much power I had in ruining my life, and conversely, making it absolutely wonderful. Everything was up to me.

Yet, you might argue, who am *I* to say you have control? Who am *I* to say you can actually turn your life around if you let yourself? Who am I to know the ins and outs of your life and that yes, you, a reader whom I do not know, can experience the transformation that I did? There's the catch: I don't know. I don't know who you are, your life situation, your goals, or your fears. Quite frankly, I don't know anything about you. I don't know your strengths or your weaknesses. I don't know why you are reading this book. I don't know why something about control and mindset resonated with you enough for you to be reading this very sentence, but I do know you picked up this book. You are a reader. You are reading my words and listening to my story. That very action—the mere action of giving this book a chance—says more than enough. It means you are *willing*. It means you are *extremely capable*. It means you are *taking action,* and action is the root of everything I am going to talk about. You are exactly where you need to be.

You are exactly where you need to be.

We return to the phrase, **"Life is what you make it."** What if we dissect that one line a little bit more, go a little deeper into what it really means.... Life is what YOU make it. What does that mean? What does it imply?

The line implies the power we have to live an extraordinary life. Yes, all of us. Me, you, your aunt, your professor, the billionaire next door, and the student struggling to make ends meet. We all have it. But the shaky waters—the uncertainty—lie in how we manifest that power, how we manifest our control, how we manifest it in the most optimal way possible in order to reap the benefits of the most incredible, magical life. How can we do just that?

Intention + action = control = change

That is our secret formula. That is the magical recipe. That is exactly what we all must bring together in order to experience what we didn't know was possible.

You are exactly where you need to be.

You took action. We all have room for improvement and a *more* optimal life. Each and every one of us. You are never too late to take action, and if we already did, there is always more to take. You have never taken enough. **We are limitless.**

The chef still has more recipes to learn and perfect.
The English teacher still has more books to read.
The millionaire still has companies to invest in.
The student still has subjects to master.
The writer still has techniques to develop.
The published professor still has research to conduct.

You are not finished. I am not finished. None of us are finished.

Rather than responding, "I know," to what someone has to say—whether or not you have heard it before—practice the responses, "great point," or "great perspective," or "wow, I hadn't looked at it that way." Because the reality is, *you didn't say what that person just said.* Their ability to formulate their thoughts as *they* did is not your work, but *theirs.* And thus, it is a *different perspective that is valuable to recognize.*

Every interaction you have is an encounter with a new perspective worthy of your attention. We all have room to listen, question, question some more, listen, and counter. **Bring back the wow factor into your life.**

Bring back the wow factor into your life.

Practice sitting in awe at everything the world has to offer.... Experience life as if it is *always your first time* experiencing that very thing.... *Bring back the excitement.* Resist your tendency to adapt. Sit in awe. Once again, *it all starts from the mind. It all starts from within.* Be easily impressed. Bring back the wow factor. Prepare yourself to unleash into the extraordinary.

Life is what you make it. This magical concept has no secrets. Until you believe this—until you come to terms with the power you have to change your life—change *will* be absolutely foolish to dream of. Because change is only a possibility once we believe in the power *we have* to create that change. The ability to recognize this power stems from an understanding of two concepts: purpose and fear. Let's begin.

PART ONE

DISCOVER & DESIRE

THE FOUNDATION OF SELF-KNOWLEDGE

Purpose. Our why. Without questioning, we live conveniently: why? Because ignorance is bliss, and completing actions merely because we have to, completing tasks because we have to, is much more convenient than questioning every decision we make. Yet living a life that is not fulfilling, in which we do not question our purpose throughout our day-to-day actions, is a waste. Living without purpose is a waste. Living on autopilot is a waste. We are not robots. We are not meant to live this way.

Getting out of bed tirelessly to the sound of a pounding alarm without thought or question as to *why* you are getting out of bed, *what* your purpose is in tackling that very day, is far too easy. Because until we understand the power in our why, any other attempt at motivation is surface-level and temporary. Purpose serves as a permanent force of motivation.

But why? Why do we do as we do? More importantly, **why do *you* do as you do?**

Our purpose can be translated into a deeper understanding of ourselves through self-knowledge.

SELF-KNOWLEDGE

Self-knowledge is a term used to describe how well you know yourself. It requires introspection, honesty, and a habit of self-reflection. In return, it provides you with a sense of understanding yourself. Once strong enough, this sense of self can push you through the greatest of disturbances and toward pondering moments of life, simply because you *know what is going on*. You are in-tune with yourself. Once you are in-tune with yourself, because you've found a cemented understanding of your purpose, everything starts to make sense.

Self-knowledge is a **foundation for movement.** You become aware of the powers you already possess and those that have not yet been unleashed. You have a starting point and a sense of direction. You become more powerful than ever before. You become unstoppable if you channel it correctly. Self-knowledge is the first step to improving your overall quality of life.

"Knowing yourself is the beginning of all wisdom."
—ARISTOTLE.

Self-knowledge has multiple sources: **social comparison, reflection on the opinions of others, introspection, an examination of your behavior** while it is occurring, or simply being actively self-aware.

"It is no coincidence that Socrates should have boiled down the entire wisdom of philosophy to one simple command: Know Yourself. This is a distinctly odd-sounding ambition. Society has no shortage of people and organizations offering to guide us around distant continents, but very few that will help us with the arguably far more important task of traveling around the byways of our own minds. Fortunately, however, there are a number of tools and practices that can help us to reach inside our minds and move us from dangerous vagueness to challenging but redeeming clarity."[4]

We will be focusing on **introspection** and becoming **actively self-aware.** Social comparison, understood in terms of Festinger's social comparison theory, explains people learn about themselves by comparing themselves to others; it uses relativity to come to conclusions.[5] There are two types of comparison—upward and downward. **Upward comparison** includes comparing ourselves to people we see to be more accomplished, leading us to feel inspired or hopeful. Yet, it also triggers feelings of inadequacy and self-inferiority. This is the greatest, most damaging impact of **social media**, as the *only comparison that exists on this platform is upward comparison.*

---

4   Botton, Alain de. *Self Knowledge.* Essay Books, n.d.

5   Psychology Today. "Social Comparison Theory." Accessed January 26, 2020. https://www.psychologytoday.com/basics/social-comparison-theory.

A 2016 study done at Scripps College examined the effects of social comparison through social media on depressive symptoms. Two-hundred participants self-reported their social media use through how many hours per day they spent on all social networking sites. Participants also answered two questions about their self-presentation and that of people they follow. Lastly, participants' social comparison was measured by the Iowa-Netherlands Comparison Orientation Measure, INCOM. Gender was also accounted for in the study. The Beck Depression Inventory was used to measure depressive symptoms.[6]

The researchers predicted upward social comparison joined by time spent on social media would be the two greatest factors influencing depressive symptoms. Their predictions were correct.

The time participants spent on social media, driven by social comparison, was correlated with the rate of clinically-diagnosed depression among the participants. Furthermore, seeing others' highlights shared (upward social comparison) had a positive correlation with the BDI for each participant.

This data is not surprising in the least.

The amount of data that positively correlates clinical anxiety, depression, and an array of social fears is sizable. More on why social media is one of the greatest inhibitors of reaching

6   Uhlir, Janet L., "Social Comparison and Self-Presentation on Social Media as Predictors of Depressive Symptoms" (2016). Scripps Senior Theses. Paper 756.

the extraordinary in Take Control of Your Devices, but for now we will focus on the power of self-knowledge outside of the relevance of others.

Downward comparison leads us to feel better about ourselves because we feel sorry for others, such as comparing your grade of ninety percent to someone who received a seventy percent on the same exam. This comparison leads you to feel better about your grade. Yet is this comparison an accurate representation of *how well you are doing?* Rather, shouldn't your comparison be to your own past exam scores, not the exam scores of others? Your improvement is what must be noted. Other people are irrelevant.

Thus, any type of social comparison is a **relative** thought process. It must be eliminated as a source of self-knowledge. Self-knowledge must come from within. You are the only being who is a part of the equation. In turn, inquiry and self-awareness are where we will focus our efforts.

Your sense of worth does *not* come from where you place the worth or value of others. Your sense of worth comes from how much *you* value yourself. Self-worth is not relative; it has no hierarchy. Do not fool yourself into believing one exists. View yourself as a single being, isolated. Do not view yourself in terms of others. This is a disturbance. Stay in tune with yourself and yourself only. The motivations of others are *not relevant to you*. What goes on in the minds of others is *not relevant to you*. Shifting your attention to the minds of others, to their motivations, is a disturbance of your peace and detracts you from *your* sense of self. This practice is a distraction.

Resist the urge for any sort of self-knowledge to originate from relativity. Do not come to conclusions about yourself using the conclusions you come to about *others*. Everything that is not blatantly stated by someone else is an *assumption*. Resist the urge to assume. Save yourself the peace of mind and energy. If every assumption you make turned out to be incorrect, would you continue to assume? Likely not. *Most of the time, our assumptions are wrong.* As much as we convince ourselves we know what is going on in other people's lives, *we don't.* The only viable solution is to focus on ourselves.

Force yourself into introspection. Force yourself into growing increasingly self-aware. Force yourself to understand the actions you take, why you take them, and what they add or detract from your state of being. Understand *what* gives you energy and what tires you. Question *what* motivates you and what doesn't light you up as much. Ask *what* you are most dearly afraid of and *why*. Come to terms with yourself. Get to know yourself.

Neglecting the need to be knowledgeable about oneself is like questioning what is missing from a puzzle without having a set of pieces in the first place. **How are you supposed to know what is missing if you don't know what already exists?**

We must know ourselves in order to know what we want.

The first step in understanding ourselves is answering the question, "But *why*?" This question underlies our purpose in our day-to-day actions, the actions we take and why we take those actions—*your* **purpose in your day-to-day actions.** Be present and come to understand what you are doing in this very moment and why you are doing it. Why are you reading this book? Why are you still reading it right now despite all the repetitive questions I'm throwing at you? What's the point? Is it to gain knowledge? Is it to improve your life? Is it because you enjoy reading? What about you is pushing you to read this very sentence?

I used to never understand the power of answering this very question. I lived on autopilot, and autopilot threw me into misery. I felt unfulfilled and empty. I was completing day-to-day tasks because I felt it was *what I had to do*, it was simply expected of me. However, **everything is a choice.** Every decision we make is a choice. We have free will. Our job is to determine *why* we make choices as we do and *what* about that exact decision connects to our underlying purpose. We most grow increasingly aware of ourselves and our actions. We must have a definitive *why* to everything we do. Autopilot must be defeated.

Autopilot must be defeated.

***

I loathed waking up each morning to go to school. I had nothing to look forward to, no mission, nothing to get me out of bed. I would wake up forcefully to my dad's nonstop, "bolansho!"—which means "get up!" in Farsi. I would go to school and count down the minutes until the last bell rang for me to run to the bus. The bus was comforting as it meant

I was leaving. It would transport me out of what felt like mental captivity and into a place of comfort, my bedroom.

I didn't know what exactly about high school disturbed me as much as it did. I enjoyed learning, I enjoyed academics. I enjoyed my classes. What was making me feel small, inadequate, limited and afraid? What was letting my mind welcome chaos? Where was my peace? Why did I feel out of control?

I didn't know. But more importantly, I didn't try to find out. I accepted this state of mind. I accepted everything. I was convinced nothing else existed than what I was feeling every day: a lack of drive, a lack of purpose, no fulfillment, fear, inadequacy.... I had no reason to better myself because it was impossible.

I forced myself into introspection. I tried to define my purpose. I tried to figure out *who I was*. Desperately.

This didn't work. I was left frustrated at my attempts. I couldn't throw a label onto myself, I couldn't define myself, so I was left feeling more lost than I was before.

The solution, although untapped in the early stages, was *coming to an understanding of myself through welcomed introspection*. The moment I *wanted* to learn about myself, the moment I *welcomed* change, the moment I *opened myself* to discomfort, was the moment I freed myself. I learned about myself, my needs, my wants, my underlying motivations. I finally figured it out.

It didn't happen overnight. Introspection was a gradual journey where time was my friend. Time was on my side. I let myself question in peace. I let myself think in peace. I welcomed introspection. I welcomed this new way of thinking. In turn, I learned more than I ever knew possible. I was *okay* with the unknown. I was *okay* with change. I had to accept the journey my mind needed to take. I said yes. I had no information on the journey. I had no map. I had to go, so I did.

When in a state of utter confusion and frustration, the last thing we will willingly do is plead guilty. We see welcoming change, a new state of mind we didn't think we would ever acquire, as inconvenient. I had to plead guilty. I had to come to terms with my life. My habits, my practices, my desires, but most importantly, *the way my mind viewed the world*. I had to come to terms with it and change what was setting me back. It all starts from within.

Why come to terms with your flaws? Why feel any sort of regret? Why bother being honest with yourself? Honesty is uncomfortable. It is frightening. It is the least convenient route to take. Yet it is the *only* route to take. We must seek discomfort in order to move forward in any medium.

I found myself living in a cycle of complaints, anger, frustration, and hardly any excitement. I accepted my life as it was. "No one cares for me, so why should I care for my own presence?", was a replayed thought. The time came for me to plead guilty.

Firstly, *what was I doing, why was I doing what I was doing,* and on top of that, *what was I doing wrong?* What was *missing?* With that information, what changes was I going to make? What was I supposed to do? *Who* and *what* were prompting these problems? What was intensifying them? What in my life, **that I can control,** is intensifying this state of mind I so desperately need to be freed from?

> *What, that I have control over, is intensifying this state of mind?*

What can I concretely change to entirely turn my life around? How can I live a consistently positive, purposeful, and passionate life? How can I grow a genuine love for life and people? How can I get to the mental space where I experience peace of mind and am free from chaos?

I was determined. I was excited to take on this journey. I had to accept a final destination, which I had not yet reached, existed. I was deprived of the spark I knew could light me up, light me up into a life of vitality, love, appreciation, and happiness. I was determined to find that spark. I had a burning desire to find that spark.

I began to reflect. I connected back to the title of this segment: purpose. I sat down and wrote down everything I did every day, including every idea I had and every person I thought about. I questioned my thought process—what took up the space in my mind? What was I constantly thinking about?

What was taking up my mental energy? Who was it? What was it? Most importantly, *why*?

I wrote down everything I did, forcing myself to grow aware of my actions. I analyzed patterns. I dug deep. I took a journey into my mind that I didn't know I was free to take.

Ask yourself, *what is going on*, and *why is this going on?*

You can only find out how to get to your destination if you know your starting point. You have no set of directions from a random point in space and time. You must travel from A to B. Your self-knowledge is your starting point. **Your journey includes coming to terms with *what* is limiting you, how to eliminate it from your life, determining *what* you desire, *optimizing* your chances at receiving those desires, and ultimately, crafting an environment that will allow for this extraordinary life to sustain itself.** It all starts from within. It all starts from viewing the world in a way that shows you are *open* to opportunity, you have *trumped fear*, and you are able to ride every wave that comes your way.

I then understood *why* I was so miserable. **I analyzed the themes in my "why."** I was now ready to take on the journey to turn my life around. I knew where I stood, so I was more informed than ever of **where I needed to be.**

This book will take you on that journey.

Let's begin.

THE FOLLOWING QUESTIONS WILL HELP YOU GET TO KNOW YOURSELF A LITTLE MORE. ANSWER IN DETAIL.

1. What is important to you?
2. Who is important to you?
3. What energizes you?
4. Who energizes you?
5. What tires you?
6. Who tires you?
7. What makes you happy?
8. Who makes you happy?
9. What do you prioritize?
10. Who do you prioritize?
11. What do you value?
12. What is your biggest strength? Biggest weakness?
13. What do you worry most about?
14. What scares you?
15. What careers interest you?
16. What do you believe in?
17. What are you good at?
18. What keeps you up at night?
19. What do you think about yourself?

How would you want someone to describe you to someone else?

Next, dissect your day-to-day actions. What decisions do you make every day, and why do you make those decisions? **What is your purpose in your day-to-day actions?**

Describe in extreme detail what a day in your life looks like. What do you do right when you wake up and what do you do moments before you fall asleep?

For example:

I wake up around 8 a.m. to my alarm. I get up and stretch and count to three, forcing myself to get out of bed by the third count. I say three things I am grateful for and why I'm excited to take on the day. I do this because it brings me peace of mind early in the morning. Because I don't go on my phone, I am still in a pure mental state. I feel disconnected and empowered. Next, I chug a glass of water, instantly hydrating my body. I grab my outfit, which I have already set up the night before, and head to the bathroom.

*I then brew a cup of coffee and force myself to write for fifteen minutes. I do this because writing early in the morning, when my mind is in its purest state, is empowering and stimulating. It inspires me to take on the day, and I find that my best ideas come during this time slot. I want to feed my soul every single day, particularly when I wake up, and I do so through writing in the early morning. **No one is forcing me to do this. These actions are solely my choices.***

DISSECTING YOUR DAY-TO-DAY ACTIONS

	Action	Reflection
1		
2		
3		
4		
5		
6		
7		
8		
9		
10		
11		
12		
13		
14		
15		
16		
17		
18		
19		
20		
21		

ANALYZE YOUR ACTIONS
What trends have you noticed? What patterns?
What habits were you not formally aware of?
What do you want to change?

WHO AND WHAT IS TAKING UP YOUR MENTAL ENERGY?

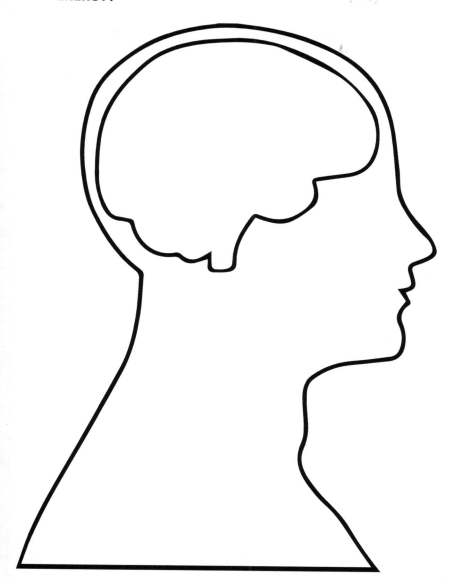

Throughout the day, pay attention to where your mind wanders off. Are you thinking about yourself? Are you thinking about others? Are you thinking about what others are thinking about you? Are you thinking about what you *need* to do? In times of despair, where does your mind go? How do you react to different situations? **What's on your mind?** Fill out this diagram in terms of *how much energy you believe you allocate to each item.*

This is your starting point. Our next step is removing one of the most damaging factors from the equation: fear.

"Expose yourself to your deepest fear. After that you are free."

—JIM MORRISON

WE ARE AFRAID

—

Now that we have gathered the puzzle pieces we already have, it is time we understand *what* is missing, and *why* it's missing.

What common denominator is stopping you from truly living your life and reaching the extraordinary? What is stopping you from bringing your desires to life? What is limiting you?

Fear.

Every opportunity we are hesitant to go after, we have given up our power to fear.
Every relationship we are hesitant to dive deeper into, we have given up our power to fear.
Every individual we are scared to speak to, we have given up our power to fear.

> *Every chance we don't take, we have given up our power to fear.*

Why is this? Why are we are so comfortable with remaining afraid? Why have we befriended fear rather than working tirelessly to remove it from our lives?

Convenience.

Fear is convenient. More often than not, it's in disguise. What does this mean? Fear is *far too powerful. It is a weapon in disguise.* This means it destroys without our notice. These exact characteristics make it more destructible than anything else we thought possible.

▌ *Fear is a weapon in disguise.*

Every excuse we make for ourselves is a hidden fear working to crush the possibility of something greater.... It's convenient to avoid applying for a job because we don't think we are qualified, or, more simply, because we are afraid of being rejected. It's convenient not to reach out to a friend because we don't think they'll want to meet up, or, more simply, because we are afraid of what they might think. Every obstacle we create for ourselves, we have given up our power to fear. More often than not, others are *not* standing in our way. **We are standing in our own way** because we have given that person—whoever they may be—the faulty power to "stand in our way."

▌ *Get out of your own way.*

Rather, *you* perceive them to be in your way. *You* have given them that power. Everything is in your head. Your mind has given someone the authority to stand in your way—where else would that authority come from? It is nonexistent until you make it existent. No one has the power they have until *you* give them that power. A coin is not of value, but a piece of metal, until we have assigned it a monetary value. Everything is a mere particle. Nothing is *anything* until we make it *something*. It's all in your head.

> *Nothing is anything until we make it something.*

Thus, your mind has created a **nonexistent dynamic**. But you, your reluctance, your fears, your hesitancy, your doubtfulness, are **completely existent**. These things stand in your way more than anything you could ever imagine. They stop you from pursuing what you find interesting and what you are passionate about. They stop you from asking for what you want. They stop you from **doing what you want to do. Fear is the underlying obstacle to nearly everything we want to achieve.**

Fear of how someone will react, fear of what someone will say—these all make us question our thoughts, our words, and our motives. In turn, we find comfort in silence. We stand idly by. We are reluctant to speak; we are reluctant to share what we think or start a conversation about something that may generate a rather controversial response.

We may be afraid to express an unpopular opinion.
We may be afraid to do something considered out of the norm.
We may be afraid to wear something that someone might not approve of.

What would you say if no one was listening? **What would you do if everything you did, said, wore, and believed was guaranteed to be idolized?** *Would you speak out more? Would you share more of what you enjoy? Would you tell more stories? Would you wear different clothing? Would you attend different events? Would you go out alone? How would your story change?*

> *The time has come to show fear what it means to be fearless.*

I used to be so ridiculously consumed by what people thought of me. I was constantly questioning my self-identity and the decisions I made. I was so consumed with blending in so that I would be accepted and fall within societal norms. My biggest fear was contradicting the rulebook, taking action against what I thought was expected of me. I couldn't imagine the response that would generate from the choices I wanted to make, so I avoided them to the extent of being miserable. Being someone you're not is absolutely miserable. It is exhausting. It is draining. The life was sucked out of me. I was so afraid.

My opinions were irrelevant, my ideas were foolish, and who I was—my character and authenticity—had no value. I was a puppet lying obedient to the judgement of the world. I was a puppet being obedient to an owner I didn't even bother to think about disobeying.

I limited myself from experiencing the wonders of life. I was held captive. I was afraid of large groups of people so I didn't get to experience the beauty of people coming together for a celebration. I would let my passions sit idly by as I was too afraid to run after them. I didn't share my voice because I was afraid of how people would respond. I was so afraid of what people would think that I shut myself down. I threw myself into misery.

FEAR OF FAILURE

———

I didn't want to take the class. It didn't interest me, I was convinced I was bad at it, everyone I knew was most definitely better at reading comprehension and writing than I was. I only enrolled in AP English Literature because I felt it was expected of me…. because everyone around me was taking it, because it was the "norm" for seniors at Palisades Charter High School. I had no motive other than feeling the course was mandatory.

Facing heavy reading assignments topped with daily discussions on what we'd read, I'd sit in class confused. I'd sit in class feeling disconnected. I had no passion for the readings, I didn't connect to them, and I struggled to dissect them as we were expected to. Writing a response to readings I had no interest in was draining. My self-esteem plummeted, and what I thought was a passion for writing diminished.

In turn, I accepted that any medium of writing I would ever take on would remain in the notes app on my iPhone, where I jotted down random thoughts, reflections, and deep introspective sessions I would occasionally have with myself. I was not equipped to welcome any type of professional writing into my life.

Yet I got to the point of writing nearly fifteen-hundred words each day without intention. The notes app on my iPhone was filled with self-reflections and teachings that served as my backbone for tackling everyday life. My writing undoubtedly stimulated me, but I still convinced myself it was lacking, it was not good enough, it wasn't meant for me.

The conclusions I made pushed me to dive into educating myself more on the topic, into coming to greater conclusions in order to better myself and those around me. Writing became my backbone, the on-call therapist who always had a solution.

But that's all it was: an escape. That's all it was ever capable of being.

A few months later, I graduated from high school and was on my way to study psychobiology at UCLA. I steadily kept my eyes on Facebook in order to see what opportunities were awaiting me, saving post after post, but never coming around to actually applying. One caught my attention: Her Campus UCLA. It was an online magazine for college women, and they were taking applications for writers for the fall quarter.

I sat there mesmerized. I wanted to be a writer for this magazine *so badly*. I wanted to write. I wanted to share my voice. I wanted to get involved. But I was *certain* I wasn't qualified. If my AP English Literature teacher hadn't made it clear already, my subconscious did. I was so afraid to fail again, to be reminded just *one more time* I wasn't meant to write. It was just another door patiently waiting to slam in my face.

I was left with a dream—dreaming to be a part of a community of creators but believing I was not capable of doing so because of prior setbacks. I knew I wasn't made for writing, knew English wasn't my strength. This exact mentality cost me years and years of my life. This fear-driven mentality. I was deathly afraid of what could go wrong; I was deathly afraid of failure in every aspect of my life.

Academics
Relationships
Opportunities
Simple day-to-day interactions
My mind

I was most terribly afraid to dig deeper into what was going on in my head; I let these voices take control of me.

"You can't do it."
"They don't like you."
"No one cares about you."
"No one loves you."
"Stop trying."
"Everyone is looking at you."
"Everyone is talking about you behind your back."
"You are a failure."
"Who even are you?"

The voice inside my head pushed me toward my demise. The voice had no truth in it; it was a stream of nonsense I was foolish enough to listen to religiously.

But for some reason, an hour before the application was due, I got on my phone, filled out the Google Doc, and submitted it on a whim.

A week later, I got a call for a phone interview. Hesitant as ever, I prepared day and night, frantically checking the time to make sure I was ready to take the call.

I'd gotten in.

I've been a feature writer for Her Campus Magazine AT UCLA for about two years now, and it has completely changed my fate; I formed a passion for writing that I forgot existed. I felt empowered. I felt heard.

I was struck with the realization that *saying* no to *yourself* was worse than being told no by *someone else*.

> *Saying no to yourself is worse than being told no by someone else.*

I was thrown into a life of YES. This sort of life took diligent practice, forcing myself out of my comfort zone, welcoming change, and welcoming the unexpected. In time, I became a yes-man. I was a fearless yes-man. I was finally free. I was liberated from the limitations I had created for myself. Fear was no longer in control. I was.

Throw yourself into a life of yes.

Free yourself. Cut the strings. Cut the nonsense.

"Do one thing every day that scares you."
—ELEANOR ROOSEVELT

I threw myself into a life of yes.

***

I was sitting in the biomedical research library at UCLA in November of 2018, studying for my biology exam, when I received an email notification about a LinkedIn message. I wasn't used to receiving random messages on LinkedIn, so I was excited, but more importantly, confused. It read:

"Hi Nicolette, I'm a Georgetown professor & have this course/ club where my students create and publish books. Expanding the club to new campuses and saw you're a writer. Any interest in writing a book and/or helping bring this club to campus -- quick 15 minute chat this week?"
—ERIC KOESTER

I sat there in awe at the message I received. "What?", I thought.

My confusion largely stemmed from the thought, "Why me?" I was only a freshman still trying to navigate the ropes of UCLA. Why was I being asked by a Georgetown professor if I was interested in taking on such a crazy project, the writing of a book? My initial thought was not to reply to the message. I wanted to crawl back into comfort and pretend I had never received it. Telling myself no was comforting; I was used to it. It seemed like the only reasonable thing to do.

Then, the realization struck: Why not? Why not *write the book*? I had so much to say after all, what was stopping me from saying it? What was stopping me from taking this one step further? A bad experience I had in English literature when I was a senior in high school? The stupid voice inside my head? The time had come to stop standing in my own way. Every limitation was in my head. Nothing was truly in existence until I let it exist.

I forced myself to seek discomfort. I reminded myself of my new mission. I said yes.

Lastly, if I knew I couldn't fail, would I take the leap? Absolutely.

> *If you knew you couldn't fail, would you take the leap?*

What leap would you take? Would you pursue a different career? Would you explore a different lifestyle? Would you make different decisions?

That's exactly what I did; I removed my fear of failure from the equation and took the leap. **Failure no longer phased me.** I became excited by it. I craved it. I was thrown into a life of "So what?" as my response to nearly any concern someone would raise. "Who cares?" became the slogan I religiously lived by. Nothing phased me. I finally understood that I had *nothing to lose.* We are all going to die someday. Living captive to fear is a waste of time. It was time to *just go for it. Every fear, every doubt, every roaming thought—it was all in my head. I had to instill in my mind that I, indeed, was fearless and had nothing to lose. I had to take control of the one thing I had absolute control over: my mind.*

Control Mindset was born.

No one starts at the finish line. We all start somewhere.

Comparing our beginnings to others' moments of near-completion is foolish, undeniably foolish because constant exposure to the successes of others is daunting. In turn, we are discouraged. Our failures consume us because we are not exposed to the failures of others; we feel alone. We feel our struggles are isolated. This creates a form of alienation.... Then it becomes ridiculously easy to give up. We lose any form of self-compassion because we feel alone—we feel it is *our* fault.

Social media does a perfect job of illuminating the end result; progress is rarely broadcasted. As a result, we are constantly being exposed to success. It forces us to question, *why do they have it so easy?* More importantly, *what am I doing wrong?*

In order to overcome this regular exposure, we must remind ourselves that *everyone starts somewhere, and no one is at the finish line.*

Rather, the greatest form of human connection is through our struggles, because *no one is cruising through the game of life. We are all fighting our own battles, even if it is impossible to believe.* You should not feel obligated to only broadcast the happy moments of your life. You should not feel obligated to make it seem like *everything is okay.*

> *The greatest form of human connection is through shared pain. So why cover it?*

Push yourself to connect with others by sharing your harder moments, allowing them to feel heard, triggering a ripple effect so that less and less people feel isolated as they battle life.

Brock Bastian, along with colleagues Jolanda Jetten and Laura J. Ferris of the University of Queensland, examined the link between pain and social bonding in a series of experiments with undergraduate students. The research suggests pain, despite its unpleasantness, may actually have positive social consequences, acting as a sort of **social glue** that fosters cohesion and solidarity within groups.[7]

---

7   Bastian, Brock & Jetten, Jolanda & Ferris, Laura. (2014). Pain as Social Glue. Psychological science. 25.

So why not try to create this social glue instead of working tirelessly to remove it through pretending pain and struggles are nonexistent? Pretending *we are doing great all the time?* Why not instead grow immensely aware of *what is going on,* but be absolutely certain we have control to *make it better?*

FACE IT. SHARE IT. WELCOME IT.

This is the exact mentality we must all exhibit: We must become obsessed with failure. We must crave it. Love it. **Welcome it.**

Failure only has the power to destroy because we have given it that power. Failure can be understood as discouraging and directive, but such an understanding is rather **wrong.** Failure is rather a *new opportunity in disguise.* It contains more within the seemingly discouraging feelings it brings.

Because rejection is only rejection if we understand it as failure. Rejection, rather, is a hidden form of **redirection.** You are being redirected to a better path, to a greater opportunity, in a disguised form that we have come to understand as failure and rejection.

Rejection is a hidden form of redirection.

Rather, we must embrace whatever form of rejection we experience because it indicates we must **redirect ourselves.** Rejection is the equivalent of your GPS system navigating you onto a different street than the one you were supposed to take.

You were supposed to take a left onto Street A, but the road was closed due to construction. So your GPS reconfigured and said to make a left on Street B. Were you rejected by Street A? No, Street A was closed. Did you fail? No. Were you redirected? Yes. Are you grateful? Of course. Who wants to deal with traffic?

> We must redefine our relationship with rejection. It's all in your head.

Think about the last time you claimed to
be *rejected*. What form did it take?

How did you feel when you were rejected?

I felt _____.

Now, understanding your rejection as redirection
in disguise, what were you redirected toward?

I was directed toward _____.

What did that redirection indicate?

My redirection indicated _____.

At one point in my life, my fear of rejection and failure was
my decision-maker. If rejection was an option, the decision
was already made for me; I opted out.... until **I redefined
my relationship with rejection.**

I was terrified of being told no. I was scared of the reper-
cussions, of threatening my self-esteem, of *what could go
wrong*. I was consumed by worry and disaster. My life felt
like it was falling apart. My relationships were suffering, my
health was deteriorating, I was getting little sleep each night,
I was glued to my phone, I was afraid of human interaction,
and I hated who I was.

When I realized I was being redirected through these
moments; I realized I had more on the horizon. The universe was screaming at me to make a change, but I couldn't

hear the screams until I let myself listen. Then, everything began to change.

It started with fear. The moment I began to actively work toward pursuing every opportunity that came my way with **little care about the end result—whether it was a success or failure—was when I regained my power.**

If I had something to say, I said it. If people responded well, great. If they didn't, so what? I was untouched by the disturbances around me.
If I had a question, I asked it. If I received an answer I wanted to hear, great. If not, oh well.
If I had a story to share, I shared it. If people resonated with it, great. If not, oh well.
If I had an outfit I really wanted to wear, I wore it. If I received compliments, great. If not, oh well.
If I felt a certain way, I expressed it. If people understood me, great. If not, oh well.

My job was no longer to please everyone around me. I was finally free. One who is free is at peace. Peace does not exist without freedom. Happiness does not exist without freedom. Life does not exist without freedom.

Think about a food you claimed to hate as a child. Back in 2007, I refused to eat peas. I said they looked funny and tasted bad. I had never had a pea in my life. In response, my mom insisted I wouldn't know if I hated peas unless I tried them. After much persistence on my mom's end, I eventually tried the peas. I loved them. I became a pea-lover. What was

I so afraid of? Having a bad taste in my mouth. My mouth rejecting the peas.

This simple analogy that we have all experienced at some point in our vegetable battles with our parents is exactly parallel to the kind of rejection and fear we encounter in our everyday lives. We never know if something won't work out unless we *take the leap.*

What decisions would you make if rejection did not exist? If you were not afraid of it?

If I were not afraid of rejection, I would...

What is stopping you from making those decisions? Spoiler: rejection DOES not exist. **Rather, it is redirection in disguise.**

IT'S ALL IN YOUR HEAD. Free yourself from the limitations you have created for yourself. Take control. Take the leap. Be free.

If you knew you could not fail ... if you were not fazed by fear or rejection, how would your story change? What type of life would you live? What type of people would you be surrounded by? What opportunities would you chase? What career would you pursue?

We will divide the fear of failure into two subcategories: failure in the **short-term,** and failure in the **long-term.** Failure in the **short-term** includes simple day-to-day decisions, such as making the decision to talk to someone you don't normally talk to, to fill out an application you would rather avoid, to start learning a new subject that is interesting but seems rather difficult, to fall into the unknown, etc. **Long-term failure** refers to larger decisions, such as in your career, for example.

FEAR OF FAILURE → SHORT-TERM

How does your fear of failure direct your short-term deci-
sion making? Think about the decisions you make on a
day-to-day basis. . . . Would they change if you were fearless?

What do you avoid?

What do you back away from?

Who do you avoid?

What are you afraid to do?

FEAR OF FAILURE → LONG TERM

How does your fear of failure direct your long-term decision making? Think about the long-term decisions you've made or are in the process of making. Would they change if you were fearless? What would you pursue if your success was guaranteed? What would your story look like?

I took the leap with peas. I took the leap starting my freshman year of college. I took the leap in writing this book. When something didn't work out and I was redirected, I was grateful. In turn, once I was on the right path, I was extremely grateful because I was informed *I was doing something right.* However, I was only informed *once I took the leap.*

So, I ask you...

Why haven't you applied to that job?

Why haven't you spoken to that person?

What are you afraid of?

Your decisions should not be made based on the possibility of success—rather, they should be made based on your *burning desire to experience that thing. Your burning desire must direct your decisions, not your fears.*

And so, *what would you do if you knew you wouldn't fail? How would your story change if failure did not phase you? What stories do you wish to tell one day? How would those stories change if you did not give up your power to fear?*

*The first step to profoundly improve your quality of life rests in your willingness to **become completely, utterly, and undeniably FEARLESS**.*

TAKE CONTROL OF YOUR FEAR OF FAILURE

METHODS

Every single day, do one thing that scares you. Start small. It can be anything: making a phone call you'd rather avoid, sending out an email you've been putting off, making plans with a friend you haven't seen in months.

Once a day, work on one thing you claim not to be good at. It can be an academic subject, an instrument, or a bad habit that you are trying to change. Let yourself fail. Experience the failure. Then, reflect on it. Has your life been extremely negatively affected because of that failure?

The next time something doesn't go your way, instead of becoming frustrated, tell yourself, "Interesting . . . let me try that again." The language you use is immensely important in how your body responds to your experiences. Didn't get a problem right on a test? Practice that response. As a result, you will calmly, and with self-compassion, guide yourself toward the right answer. It is okay. Failure is okay. Welcome it.

The next time someone asks you a question where you seek comfort in avoiding it or saying no, say without hesitation, without any questioning, without any fear, "YES!" See where this answer can take you.

The moment the little voice inside your head creeps up, respond to it immediately with, "Okay . . . and?" This tactic is so powerful. You are completely dismissing its power by being nonreactive. Non-reactivity is your power. You don't need to fight back. Rather, acknowledge it. Let it know it's being heard. Then, dismiss it by rising above it.

AFFIRMATIONS
I...

CHECK INS & ADJUSTMENTS

What is working and what isn't? How do you feel? What adjustments can you make? Do you feel more liberated? Evaluate. Edit your story as much as you want. After all, this story is yours.

FEAR OF AUTHENTICITY

———

I looked in the mirror, questioning the girl staring back at me. She was wearing an outfit she was not comfortable in; her hair was styled in accordance with the most recent trend, and she was wearing makeup because she thought it was normal for girls her age who wanted to be liked by boys. The girl in the mirror was a stranger.

She was afraid. She was afraid of what people would say if she went to school looking the way she did. The way she expected people to react was replaying in her head. The judgement of the world was waiting to be thrown onto her shoulders. She was ready to go to war and lose. She was ready to be defeated.

I continued to look in the mirror, moving my body around, paying close attention to all of my features in disgust, frustrated as to why I looked the way I did, why my body was shaped the way it was.

I was convinced no one would like me if I wore the clothing I liked, if I wore my hair how I liked it, and, most importantly, if I went to school with no makeup on. The girl in the mirror lived religiously by the opinions of others, by her burning desire to be accepted, to fit in. The girl in the mirror was a stranger. The girl in the mirror was stuck. She was trapped.

> *I was forcing myself to play the role of a character that I did not audition for.*

Why is it so hard to follow the most commonly shared piece of advice: "Be yourself?"

From a young age, we are told it. The immediate response to any form of panic or stress is: "Don't worry, just *be yourself!*" But what does that really mean, and why isn't it practiced as much as it is preached?

Why do we become less and less comfortable in our skin to the point that we require the external validation and approval of others to be openly, proudly, and *loudly* authentic, *if anything?*

Why does it take this much effort? Why does it require the work of others? Why is it a *team effort?* WHY IS IT SO HARD?

We are afraid to be ourselves. We are deathly afraid to be authentic.

In "Let's Face It, We're Deathly Afraid of Authenticity," Kathy Caprino, writer and speaker, reveals how inauthentic the vast majority of people on this planet are, not because they want to be liars or withholders, **but because they're deathly afraid to be real.**[8]

Caprino further explains how this phenomenon exists: "We're taught it's not safe to share the realness of our challenges, and we're scared to be ostracized and judged. And from a societal perceptive, it isn't safe. We are scorned, rejected, and alienated when we do."[9]

There is a comfort in being the person you believe you are expected to be. There is a comfort in fitting in. There is a comfort in remaining on the surface. We are comforted by being the person we think people will accept, the person who isn't susceptible to judgement or hate. We are comforted by fooling ourselves into the idea we are protected.

In high school, the noise of the outside world consumed every bit of my mental energy.

I would make up theories in my head of what people were saying. I would become so invested in bringing these theories to life that they would become my reality. I was convinced I was hated and on everyone's minds in the lowest regard. Little did I know, everyone is too busy thinking about

---

8   "Let's Face It—We're Deathly Afraid Of Authenticity." Accessed December 26, 2019. https://www.forbes.com/sites/kathycaprino/2016/09/18/lets-face-it-were-completely-afraid-of-authenticity/#474f0ce56b68.

9   "Let's Face It—We're Deathly Afraid Of Authenticity." Accessed December 26, 2019. https://www.forbes.com/sites/kathycaprino/2016/09/18/lets-face-it-were-completely-afraid-of-authenticity/#474f0ce56b68.

themselves to be focused on anyone else to the extent we believe they are.

It came to a point where I deactivated my Instagram because I was so out of touch with the person I was portraying on social media. I was lost. But to a greater extent, I was so afraid of what people would think of the near-character I had created for the internet to see.

I was consumed by the noise of the world.

I was to blame. I gave the *noise* of the world **too much power**.

We have given the noise of the world—the thoughts, judgements, and streams of *jealousy* from others—the power to *change who we are, the power to make us feel uncomfortable in our own skin, the power to make us feel ashamed for our true selves, and the power to make us feel ashamed for the most beautiful versions of ourselves: our most authentic selves.*

> *Our authenticity has been stripped by the noise of the world.*

I call it noise due to the nature of its *disturbance. The thoughts and negative responses from the outside world are a disturbance. They create chaos in our minds. They are consuming. They need to be silenced.* Only then will the light inside of us be able to shine. Yet *will the noise ever be silenced? Will it ever be nonexistent?* Absolutely not.

THIS NOISE ONLY HAS POWER ONCE WE GIVE IT POWER. EVERYTHING STARTS FROM WITHIN. NOTHING IS ANYTHING UNTIL WE MAKE IT SOMETHING. WE MUST NOT MAKE THE NOISE OF THE WORLD ANYTHING. WE MUST SIMPLY LET IT EXIST.

How can we let our souls breathe? How can we let the purest version of our selves unleash into the world? How can we let our flames stay on fire *forever*?

We must instill a burning desire to be authentic, tirelessly fight for our individuality, and *silence the noise by overpowering it. We must be louder.*

Why is it so easy to **jump into character** once we feel uncomfortable? Jumping into character is parallel to jumping into some sort of safety net. This artificial front, this character, exists as a defense mechanism against the **fear of being accepted and liked.**

Until you reach the point where every decision you make is, without question, for *yourself*, you have fallen subject to your fear of authenticity. You must push to overcome.

Why suffer through the discomfort and uncertainty of who you truly are when you can adjust to your environment in order to please those around you? It seems like the only viable solution to changing environments: tweak who we are in order to be liked, tweak who we are in order to fit in. This solution is convenient and comfortable. However, your true self suffers as the projection you create only continues to fool those around you, ultimately suffocating your soul more and more, carefully building the trap for your demise. This habit is not sustainable. Authenticity is.

The only way to become unapologetically authentic is through diligent practice. We must constantly ask ourselves two very important questions and make instant changes according to our answers.

1. **Am I making this decision for myself or for others?**
   a. Am I making this decision to please someone else?
   b. Am I making this decision because it is expected of me?
   c. Am I making this decision because this is normal?
   d. Am I making this decision because I am afraid of what people might think if I were to do it differently?

2. **Am I letting fear get in the way of my authenticity?**
   a. Am I afraid of what people will think if I do this thing?
   b. Am I afraid this is not expected of me?
   c. Am I afraid people will think I'm stupid?
   d. Am I afraid people will talk behind my back?
   e. Am I afraid people will judge me?

If you are making decisions for others, retract immediately. Make it your instinct to retract and remake your decision. Train yourself. Diligently practice. Become unbelievably self-aware.

If you are letting your fear of judgement get in the way of authenticity, cross the line. Seek discomfort in that very moment. Then, reflect. How do you feel? Do you feel that you are being the absolute purest form of yourself? Liberated? Uncomfortable? Scared? Different? Keep track of this feeling every time you cross the line and break the rules. In time, you will no longer have a reaction. Being authentic will be as instinctual as drinking water when you are thirsty. It will become human nature.

> *People are going to judge you no matter what. Not everyone is going to like what you are doing. Stop trying to please everyone. Please yourself first.*

Take two groups: Group A is composed of people who have accepted you for who you are. Group B is composed of people who make you feel ashamed for who you are. So, your immediate response is to seek acceptance from Group B. You want to change their minds. You want to be liked. You try to tweak who you are in order to be accepted, in order to fit in. Great—you finally feel like you're a part of Group B. Now what? Group A steps back. They no longer feel connected to you. Who benefitted from this experiment? No one.

Group A lost a member whom they cared for.

Group B gained a member who is inauthentic around them.

You have sacrificed your authenticity.

No one won.

> *You can't please everyone. And once you try to, you lose your sense of self, and you lose those who have accepted you for who you are in the first place. You lose.*

In your lifetime, you are only going to continue to please the people who have already accepted you for who you are. You are not going to change the minds of those who have turned against you, who are bothered by your fire. You must *forget them. Leave them out of your striving for excellence.*

When starting a business, the first step is to identify *who* your consumers are. Your audience. As a business, your job is to cater to those specific consumers, to their needs. For example, let's look at vegan cheese companies. Yes, you read that correctly. Vegan cheese companies manufacture and sell vegan cheese. Their target consumers are typically vegan and lactose-intolerant individuals. They are *not* trying to sell their product to dairy-lovers. This strategy would be foolish.

You are no different. Why waste your time trying to please those who *do not understand you*, those who *do not believe in you*, those who do not *accept you for who you are?* You have already filtered out the consumers who are not interested in your products, and thus you spend no time trying to please that select group. Rather, you continue to perfect your craft, and the audience who chose you in the beginning will continue to choose you. Thus, you have no logical reason to *ever change to please anyone.* Your audience has already chosen you.

The vegan cheese company would never try to sell to dairy-lovers, just as you should never try to please people who do not want to be pleased. Let yourself attract your audience. Don't fight it. Don't look for another audience. Stick to yours. Find your noise. Let it silence the disturbances around you. This is how you will win. Be louder.

We must grow resilient toward the noise of the world. This is the only way to take back our authenticity and live with peace and joy. Otherwise, our minds become overloaded with the chaos that stems from *the power we have wrongfully given to the voices in our head and around us.*

Only one you exists; this is your power. This power of authenticity is as loud as you let it be, and it can silence the hatred and jealousy of the world around you in an *instant* if you let it, if you give it the power to silence.

- When do you feel most authentic? Where are you? Who are you with? Are you alone?
- What about that environment makes you feel the purest form of yourself?
- What environment makes you feel the least authentic? When and where are you most uncomfortable? Who are you around?
- How would you behave if no one was watching?
- Who would you be if no one was watching?

Lastly,

Who would you be if all you did was constantly met with acceptance and praise?

Would you feel more comfortable in your skin? Would you proudly show off your true self? Would you be afraid to be who you *really* are—the person you are when no one is watching, the person you are around your dearest loved ones?

Morph the most powerful version of yourself—your authentic self—into every environment you take on every single day. No person, no place, no time has the power to dim your light.... to blow out your flame ... to rob you of your authenticity ... unless you give that person or thing the power to do so. Hold onto your power. Hold onto your authenticity.

You must be louder. You must channel your inner flame and let it burn.

Your authenticity is your power. Unleash it.

PROMISE YOURSELF TO BE
AUTHENTIC. PROMISE TO ...
GROW INDIFFERENT TO THE NOISE OF THE WORLD,
SILENCE IT WITH YOUR NOISE FROM WITHIN, AND
UNLEASH YOUR AUTHENTICITY.
UNLEASH YOUR POWER.

You might be comforted by being the person you believe you are expected to be, comforted by fitting in. You might be comforted by remaining on the surface, by being the person you think people will accept, who isn't susceptible to judgement or hate.

TAKE CONTROL OF YOUR AUTHENTICITY

METHODS

Every action you take, everything you say, every decision you make—ask yourself if that decision aligns with your purpose and your purpose only. If it does, wonderful. If it doesn't, realign. Re-evaluate your decision.

Ask yourself, what would you do if you were the only person on this planet? If no one was watching? How would your story change if you were alone here?

What decisions would you make if you knew everything you did was met with support and praise?

Take note of your environment when you feel particularly energized or dimmed. When you are energized, when you are unapologetically yourself, where are you? Who are you around? Take note and maximize the presence of those people and those places in your life. Go there more. Spend time with those people more. In turn, you will be forced into authenticity. In time, you will only know authenticity. Take control of your environment to bring change.

Every morning, write down three things you love about yourself. The practice may be uncomfortable at first, but force yourself into a mindset of self-compassion. Compliment yourself. Speak to yourself as you would to a friend who needs uplifting. Then, that following evening, ask yourself if those three qualities were sprinkled into the world that day. If they weren't, ask yourself why. You are your best self when you are your most authentic, when your most beautiful qualities are highlighted. The moment you have lost yourself, come to terms with your deviation and push tirelessly to return to your center.

AFFIRMATIONS
I...

CHECK INS & ADJUSTMENTS

What is working and what isn't? How do you feel? What adjustments can you make? Do you feel more liberated? Evaluate. Edit your story as much as you want. After all, this story is yours.

FEAR OF VULNERABILITY

———

Everything is a game. Presenting glamour, success, and perfection is seemingly mandatory. Any type of struggle, uncertainty, or blatant truth is not welcomed, and in turn, is feared. Admitting defeat is forbidden. Accepting wrong-doing is a sign of weakness. We must protect ourselves in order to win this game. Sharing our emotions or coming to terms with a pressing feeling pushes us further from the finish line. Opening up our hearts is forbidden. Everything is a game, and everyone is trying to win, but the race to the top is slowly killing us all.

WE NEED TO WELCOME VULNERABILITY. The winner is not the one who is always right, who lives in strict accordance with their fear of sounding stupid or wrong, who is desperately afraid to lose, who constantly struggles to say how they feel, who avoids coming to terms with their needs, who avoids their problems to the extent that they creep up and defeat them in time, or who runs away. The winner is the person who OVERCOMES. **The winner is the one who WELCOMES VULNERABILITY.**

I used to live religiously by believing I had to be like everyone else in order to be accepted, in order to dodge any form of judgement. I was afraid to feel. I was afraid to come to terms with my needs, with what my mind and body were desperately trying to tell me. I convinced myself *I was fine,* recognizing any of my body's cues was a sign of weakness, *trying to help myself was a sign of weakness.* I was afraid to help myself. In turn, I suffered beyond measure.

"Only in embracing our true nature, at our deepest core level, as emotional, vulnerable, and feeling beings are we able to tap our resilient inner strength."[10]

If I asked a stupid question, I was ashamed for hours. If I lost at something, my self-esteem plummeted. If I let down my guard, I was defeated. If I came to terms with my feelings, I was thrown into distress. If I dealt with my problems, they became real.

This mindset, this extremely deep-rooted set of fears, threw me into an isolated room with a door half open that I would never dare walk through.

In time, I became a ticking time bomb waiting to explode. So much was inside me that I was so afraid to unleash that it ended up exploding right in front of me. When it did, I couldn't handle it. I didn't know what to do.

---

10   Tiny Buddha. "Overcoming the Fear of Vulnerability & Unlocking Your Power," August 15, 2014. https://tinybuddha.com/blog/overcoming-fear-vulnerability-unlocking-power/.

Running away from our problems is convenient. Pretending they don't exist, refusing to come to terms with what we have experienced, is convenient. Not coming to terms with what we desperately need to accept is convenient. **This way of thinking is dangerous.** Nothing is more beautiful than raw, human connection through shared vulnerability. Nothing is more beautiful than dismissing the need to constantly protect ourselves from the outside world. Nothing is more beautiful than being utterly, absolutely, and completely free, all channeled through a power we each have but are terrified to unleash: our vulnerability. We must collectively work to welcome vulnerability back into our lives, allowing us to enrich ourselves and those around us in every single way possible.

Your vulnerability is your power, nothing less.

Your vulnerability is what allows you to connect with people in ways you would not know were possible otherwise. Your vulnerability is what will allow you to drastically improve all of your relationships; shared vulnerability is the most profound way to create and tighten a bond.

More importantly, your vulnerability is what allows you to *take care of your mind and body.* Your vulnerability is what allows you to take a step back and *let yourself heal.* Your vulnerability is a reminder you are not supposed to be unstoppable. It is okay to take a step back. It is okay to pause. It is okay to heal.

Your vulnerability is what opens you up to the realms of self-improvement, toward becoming the best version of yourself. Your vulnerability is what will allow you to learn more than ever before by asking questions you were otherwise afraid to ask. Your vulnerability is what opens up streams of opportunities you otherwise did not know existed. Your vulnerability allows you to finally experience life in its greatest abundance. Your vulnerability allows you to be YOU.

"Vulnerability is the only authentic state. Being vulnerable means being open for wounding, but also for pleasure. Being open to the wounds of life means also being open to the bounty and beauty."

—STEPHEN RUSSELL

Reaching true vulnerability is reaching absolute peace with oneself and the world around. Vulnerability is mandatory in order to live an extraordinary life. Reaching true vulnerability means easily coming to terms with oneself and one's surroundings, regaining all power over what would otherwise phase you.

THE VULNERABILITY LADDER
I finally climbed the vulnerability ladder. I finally freed myself.

The vulnerability ladder is an analogy for the two steps you can take to welcome vulnerability back into your life. The first step is external vulnerability, and the second step is internal vulnerability. I will explain each on the next page.

With each step I took, I felt more and more empowered. I felt I was empowering those around me. I felt pure and fulfilled. I urged my friends to climb the ladder with me. I call it a ladder for the further up you climb, the more and more free you feel. Imagine climbing a ladder to the top of a mountain. Imagine finally reaching the peak. Close your eyes; how do you feel? At the peak of the mountain, your lungs are filled with clean air and your body is invigorated by the energy flowing inside of you. You are at peace. That is how the top of the vulnerability ladder feels. You will feel free. You will feel at peace. Climb with me.

LEVEL ONE: EXTERNAL VULNERABILITY

External vulnerability encompasses freeing yourself from your fear of expression.

If you miss someone, tell them. Pick up the phone and let them know. Or better yet, ask to make plans that day. Let them know how much you miss them. What is stopping you from doing so?

If you love someone, tell them. Tell them how much you love them. Better yet, attach their name when you do. Hearing one's name is one of the most beautiful, intimate words someone can hear. What do you have to lose? Life is too short to keep your love contained. Call your parents. Tell them you love them. Be unconditional with the love you give, and you will receive it unconditionally in return. Fill yourself with love.

If you think someone is doing something right, tell them. Congratulate them. Praise them. Make them feel great. A compliment is free and has an incredibly lasting effect. Make someone feel amazing through a few simple words.

If you need help, ask for it. Nothing is wrong with asking for help. You are not supposed to know everything. We learn through others. Put your pride away. Asking is admirable. No, you don't sound stupid. Ask the damn question. You have nothing to lose.

If you don't know something, simply say, "I don't know." Don't feel the need to pretend. Who are you trying to impress? What are you trying to prove? Free yourself and *own* the fact that you do not know something, but want to learn!

LEVEL TWO: INTERNAL VULNERABILITY

Become one with your emotional present and past. Be vulnerable with *yourself*. Don't feel the need to pretend you are not *feeling* a certain way. Don't feel the need to pretend your feelings do not exist, to brush them aside, to shove them under the rug. Come to terms with your feelings. Everything you feel is valid. Every single thing.

If you aren't feeling good, **take a step back. Come to terms with your emotions.**

If you need something, recognize those needs, and meet them.

If your body is trying to tell you something, **listen.**

TAKE CONTROL OF YOUR VULNERABILITY

METHODS

ADMIT when you are wrong.

QUESTION when you DON'T KNOW.

If you don't know, don't try to ACT like you DO!

SHARE how you feel. You don't know how much that one act of bravery can help someone else.

BECOME ONE with your struggles.

LOSE the desire to showcase GLAMOUR → NONE OF US HAVE IT EASY.

Rather, STRIVE to showcase HONESTY, INTEGRITY, THE PROCESS, THE UNKNOWN, YOUR STRUGGLES. . . . CONNECT WITH OTHER PEOPLE THROUGH THE GREATEST MEDIUM: YOUR VULNERABILITY.

AFFIRMATIONS
I...

CHECK INS & ADJUSTMENTS

What is working and what isn't? How do you feel? What adjustments can you make? Do you feel more liberated? Evaluate. Edit your story as much as you want. After all, this story is yours.

YOUR FEARLESS PURSUIT OF THE EXTRAORDINARY

—

No one has the power to pose as any sort of limit unless you give them that power, which stems from your *inability* to *believe in yourself.*

Everything you might believe to be a limit or an obstacle, you have created in your mind. **Nothing exists until you make it exist. It's all in your head.**

Everything just *is*. But what *is* anything without the might you have given it?

What is a kitchen without *your* understanding you cook in there? A kitchen can be *anything*. It just *is*. Until you gave it that function, it was just a room with appliances and whatnot.

Everything has *might* because you let it, because of your mind. You are giving that *thing* power. You have control over what is what.

Everything is a particle, after all, a particle with no value or meaning. The meaning comes from YOU. You have the ability to assert. A quarter is only a piece of metal until we assert it has the value of $0.25.

Mindset shifts spark reality shifts. Everything is in your head.

The actions you want to make are finally made. The thoughts you want to share are shared. The experiences you want to experience are experienced. You are no longer your own limiting factor, and so nothing else in this world is in return. I will go more in-depth on this concept in The Power of Perspective.

Thus, you have *no internal limits besides the ones you make up for yourself. Nothing exists unless you have accepted its existence, until it has been recognized. Internal limits are not any different.*

You are not limited. You are limitless. Chase after your burning desires like no one is standing in the way, because no one is standing in the way except your inability to believe that you are, indeed, limitless. Be limitless. Be fearless. Do it.

You are unstoppable. You are invincible. You are one of the most powerful forces on this earth. And anyone who gets in your way is only there because you have placed them there.

> *"Anyone who gets in your way is only there because you have placed them there. And once they are placed, they are very easy to remove."*

When you are driving on the road and some sort of blockage appears—whether a rodent roaming across the street or a pothole—your immediate instinct is to drive around it, correct? The entire street works together to make sure everyone can drive around it safely. You wouldn't turn around, but rather work around it.

Life's obstacles are no different. We must accept they're there. They must be acknowledged. Then, we must move around them. In this case, your movement is you rising above the obstacle, for it does not have any power—it is empty—without the power you give it through how you respond to it. Take away the power you have given your obstacles. Overpower them.

INSTILL A BURNING DESIRE TO BE FEARLESS

As we continue to connect to the theme of fear, we must assess *how* we will handle it—how we will remove it from our lives in order for such an achievement to be as fulfilling as possible. Because sure, we all desire to overcome our fears; imagine how powerful we become once we do so! But this desire also seems so readily used: "How can I overcome my fear of heights," or, "How can I stop being so afraid of change?" Yet to what degree do we pursue these desires? Do we actively work to become fearless?

The answer is no.

In order to do so, we must instill a **burning desire to be fearless**. We must be **ridiculously intentional** with what we want to achieve, with what we want to experience. Otherwise, we are left with a loop of desires and a sense of discouragement from what we perceive as failure.

Becoming fearless must be a **priority in our lives** in order for fear to be recognized as **a priority to get rid of.** We can't dispose trash that hasn't yet been recognized as something to be thrown away. We might have a lot of clothes we want to get rid of, or candy wrappers sitting on our desks, but they won't be taken out until they are ready to be disposed. You have to physically get up, pick up those items, the clothing and the wrappers, and dispose of them. Otherwise, you sit surrounded by what I like to call old trash; old because it's been sitting there, trash because you know you don't want it in your life. It's old trash. You know you need to get rid of it, but you don't. Not doing so is convenient. Your fear is no different. You are aware of it, it creeps up behind you every single day, yet have you taken the necessary steps to *throw it out*?

Living in fear, accepting this way of living, is convenient. Why bother trying to figure out what you are afraid of and how you are going to remove that element from your life when you can just sit idly by and accept your state of being?

It all starts with the burning desire to be fearless.

It can't just be any desire. It must be a **burning desire**. This means we must live every single day to push ourselves closer and closer to a fearless state of mind. How do we do that?

The **desire to be fearless** is the foundation for bringing about **actual change** and **overcoming our fears—overcoming what stops us from experiencing what we deserve to experience.**

But the question lies in a number of questions: *What are your fears? What are the obstacles? Who are they? What are they? Where do they reside?* The answers to these questions are not sitting right in front of us. But rather, they are highlighted in the trend of our reactions and actions. What actions do we usually take most often? How do you react to situations that don't go your way? To situations that are seemingly uncomfortable and scary?

We must first remind ourselves of the **power of the process.** No change is instantaneous. All change is gradual and comes with time; ach change is unique to each and every one of us. The time has come to create our Fearless Goal Sheet (more on formal goal setting later). In terms of knocking fear out, we must start with being **intentional** and **goal-driven.** That is the only way we can bring about concrete change. Let's begin.

Now that you know **what fears are stopping you, what do you want to experience?** In simpler terms, what would you do if you knew.…

- You knew you would not fail, knew success was guaranteed?

- You knew everyone would love you for who you were, knew your actions were always met with acceptance?
- Your vulnerability was always taken as strength, not weakness?

What would you do if you *knew* every action you take, every decision you make, everything you do would just work out?

We will dive into answering these three questions. We will divide them into different chunk in order to knock out fear nearly **everywhere**. You will answer these three questions for every little chunk of your life.

- Academics
- Career
- Relationships
- Hobbies
- Social Interactions
- Family

Now that you know what you *would* do if fear of failure, authenticity, and vulnerability **did not exist**, you need to **envision yourself pursuing these very desires and bringing them to life by creating your Fearless Goal Sheet.** The types of goals you set, the language you use and how consistent you are with using it are *imperative* to how much it can help you, to the change it can bring you. YOU have control over this sheet. Take control and become fearless. Let's begin.

First,

WHAT DO YOU WANT? WHAT DO YOU DESIRE?

Truly, what are your most **burning desires?** What do you envision for yourself? What do you want out of life?

These desires are not *goals*, so they do not need to be specific and come with deadlines. But rather, they must exist for *your* own good. This is *your* life. What do you want out of it?

This question is complex and has many components. We will begin by breaking it up into the chunks mentioned on the previous page. Here, we are **building our vision through burning desires.** We will envision the life we want for ourselves. Every aspect of it. Just focus on what you envision. Not how you are going to get there, not what it takes, not what is feasible and what seems impossible right now. Your focus is *where you want to be* and *what you want to experience*.

- *Your Academics*
  - In your academic life, what do you want to achieve? What do you want to take from your education? Why are you even going to school in the first place? Because you are forced to? Or because you want to learn? How successful do you truly want to be in your academic career? Is it important to you? How important is it to you? What do you want for yourself? If you could pick any academic career and *guarantee* a set of results for yourself (grades, professors, study habits, etc.), what would that be? How would you describe it to someone granting your wish?
- *Your Career*
  - What do you want from your career? In what way do you want to grow? What type of environment do you

want to work in? With what types of people? With what types of opportunities? Where? What type of hours do you want to work? What is the ideal work-life for you? If you could pick *any* career and *completely* choose *every single aspect of that career life*, how would you describe it? How would you describe it to someone granting your wish?

- *Your Relationships*
  - We will divide relationships up into your immediate circle of family, your immediate circle of friends, your extended circle of family, your extended circle of friends, your academic network, your career network, and everyone else: your acquaintances, neighbors you don't talk to often, etc. What do you want from these relationships? If you could control every relationship you had and make it exactly what you wanted, what would they be like? Who would you want to be closer to? Who would you want to be distant from? Who do you want in your life? Who don't you want in your life? Who is important to you?
- *Your Hobbies*
  - What current hobbies do you want to devote more time toward? What hobbies do you keep thinking about picking up, but never have? Write every single one of them down. Do you want to learn the guitar? Piano? Read more often? Write more?
- *Your Health*
  - What about your health? What foods are you consuming? How do you feel about what you eat? What would be the most optimal diet for you? Would you go vegan if you felt you would succeed and never give in? Would you go to the gym every day if you

had one of the most exclusive memberships of all time? Do you want to live long? Do you want to work out more? Do you want to eat better? What do you envision for your health?

- *Your Mind*
  - What do you want for your mental space? What do you want to change? Do you want to experience peace and ease? Do you want to be constantly grateful rather than filled with complaints? Do you want to focus better? What do you want that your mind can provide for you?

YOUR DESIRES ENVISIONED

Write down every single one of your desires. Draw them out. Visualize them. Do whatever it takes to envision what you want to experience, what you want out of life, even if it all seems impossible. What is the *ideal* life for you? **What type of life would you be utterly obsessed with? Don't think practically. Be a dreamer. Push yourself past the limits you have created for yourself.**

WHAT TYPE OF LIFE WOULD YOU BE OBSESSED WITH? DESCRIBE IT! GO INTO HEAVY DETAIL. EVERY LITTLE PIECE AND BIT OF IT! EVEN WRITE DOWN WHATEVER YOU THINK IS IMPOSSIBLE TO EVER HAVE IN FRONT OF YOU!

		What do you desire?	Visualize Your Desire
1	Academics		
2	Career		
3	Relationships		
4	Hobbies		
5	Health		
6	Mind		

"We all have the extraordinary coded within us, waiting to be released."

—JEAN HOUSTON

PART TWO

MANIFEST & UNLEASH

TAKING CONTROL, PIECE BY PIECE

Now that we have discussed the power of fear and your ability to overcome it by carefully crafting and using your control card, we will shift gears to the places you *can* strategize and *take control* in order to optimize your journey and destination, both within and above the realms of your mind. This is the how portion of your journey. You have already stated what you want. You have already come to terms with what is stopping you from getting there. Now, the time has come to optimize, to align everything perfectly so you are the ultimate candidate to live the most incredible life possible—a life of peace, stability, love, and success—all by simply *taking control*. Let's begin.

TAKE CONTROL OF
YOUR HABITS

——

Your habits are your secret weapon. Your habits are what determine how your energy and attention are manifested, the absolute foundation of your life. Your attention and your energy make up who *you* are. **You are your attention. You are your energy.** What you direct your attention toward consumes your mind, and your mind is *who you are*. Where you spend your energy determines what is of value to you, and how you value yourself. Each of these are determined by your habits: the actions you take on a daily basis, the tendencies you have formed.

Your habits must direct your attention and your energy in such a way to protect your peace, maintain your alignment, and strictly move you forward. Your habits must be managed in such a way that they are in *your favor.* Your habits are YOURS, after all. They are your decisions; they are the actions you take on a regular basis. They must optimize your way of living in every way possible; they must put you ahead.

Your habits are *who you are*. You must form habits so aligned with your purpose and mission you are able to stay grounded and centered even amidst the greatest cloud of chaos. You must take control of your habits.

THE HABITS OF THE MIND

We will split the discussion up into two types of habits: **habits of the mind and habits of the body.** The habits of the mind revolve around the tendencies of your thoughts: how you react to certain situations, how you approach the unexpected, your habit to self-reflect, your habit to be self-aware, your habit to self-heal, whether you make decisions to protect your peace and instill free will or are mindless in your pursuits. These tendencies can also include how you react to chaos, whether you allow it to consume you or remain unbothered by the inevitable disturbances of the world. Most importantly, your habit to go after what you want, to instill burning desires, to take care of yourself ... I call these habits because these tendencies can be *formed*. They are malleable. You are able to *change the way your mind works by creating new habits. It is called a habit because it takes time to form; new perspectives and ways of thinking do not come overnight. They take practice. They take reminders. Each and every one of us is capable of morphing our minds to propel us forward with every thought we think and every instance of understanding we exhibit.* On the contrary, the habits of the body are physical actions we take and decisions we make. These include the *Atomic Habits* that are readily preached by the most successful leaders and entrepreneurs of the world, for example. I will not be focusing on the habits of the body, for these physical habits are decisions which are outside the realm of this book.

The Control Mindset is a result of the collection of the habits of the mind, a mindset in which you are constantly aware of the *control you have over your mind*; you have the control to change, to instill burning desires and bring them to life, to unlock your full potential. Once that control is discovered, the power you have in living a truly wonderful, fulfilling life is pressingly obvious. Everything starts with the mind, and, more importantly, gearing the mind toward forming these newfound perspectives, understandings, and practices. Your habits will take you there.

I will be discussing three principal habits of the mind. Every other practice and lesson I have discussed throughout this book can also be translated as a habit of the mind. You must determine which practices are of greatest value to you and place them into the realm of habits you want to work toward. For example, you must form a *habit* of saying yes. You must form a *habit* of protecting your peace. You must form a *habit* of being authentic. Every type of change you want to see starts with the formation of a habit. Habits are formed through consistency and patience. We must be consistent and patient when trying to bring about any type of change.

> *Every type of change you want to experience starts with the formation of a habit.*

THE THREE PRINCIPAL HABITS OF THE MIND
THE HABIT OF CONTROL
THE HABIT OF PERSPECTIVE
THE HABIT OF NOTABLE INSIGNIFICANCE

THE HABIT OF CONTROL

You must form the habit of understanding that you indeed *do have control over your mind.* You have control to direct your life as you wish. You have the control to bring change, to maximize what brings you peace, joy, and fulfillment, and to minimize what does the opposite. You must form the habit of constantly understanding, from within, that *you do have control.* This means no longer leaving room for complaints or leaving room to conclude you have "bad luck," and that "you can't do anything about it." ... for you CAN. You CAN do something about it. You DO have control.

Yet, it *also* requires you to understand where you *don't have control* and removing your energy and attention from such people and experiences. Where might this be? Where do you no longer have control? If you *feel* you are *over-investing,* if you cannot concretely come to a *solution,* then you must rise instead of trying to strategize toward some end result. *If you don't have control, you must remove your attention and energy.* You must form this habit of understanding, for then you are free, you are liberated. You will begin to only put your energy toward *what you can change,* and free yourself from *what you cannot.* Chaos will be limited. You will constantly experience peace of mind. Everything will make sense.

You have the control to train your mind in order for it to function in *your favor*. Your mind is extremely powerful. You must take advantage of it.

THE HABIT OF PERSPECTIVE

Nothing is anything until we make it something. Everything *is* because we have given it power to *be*. Power is relative. It all starts from within. We must form a habit of having a perspective that embraces everything around us, giving power to what *empowers us* and removing power from *what hinders* us. This can be done through an adjustment of our perspective: how we perceive what is in front of us.

> *We must maximize what empowers us and minimize what hinders us.*

We are all particles. Nothing is anything until we make it something. A coin is a piece of metal until we give it some sort of monetary value. A tree is only a tree until we give it the power to strike us with beauty and awe. A shirt is only a shirt until we give it the power to make us feel confident because it is our favorite shirt. Why *not* be easily impressed? Why *not* be amazed by life's simplest treasures, such as the sun setting or a streak of light peeking through on a particularly gloomy evening? Why give someone the power to make you feel small when you can empower yourself to feel strong? Why give a piece of paper, such as an exam or assignment, the power to induce stress when you could view it simply, as a piece of paper?

How we perceive something determines its impact and value on our lives.

Perception determines impact. Thus, we must adjust our perception to we receive what we need to receive and can be protected from what no longer serves us. We must protect ourselves as best we can, and this can be achieved through how we perceive our existence along with what we are surrounded by.

Your perception is your reality.

***

It begins with the understanding that everything around us is a gift: every opportunity, every experience, every individual. Many of these gifts are in disguise and take unfolding to reach, yet if we are able to transform our lens so everything around us has an essence of magic to it, our lives can become fulfilling and more beautiful than ever before.

The secret lies in the power our mentality and mindset have to morph our reality. Everything is as it is because our perception makes it that. Nothing else. It all begins with YOUR mind. If you're doing homework thinking you hate it, thinking it's so boring, then your experience is going to be dreadful. But if you do your homework thinking chemistry is your favorite subject, thinking this is what you *love* to do, then your experience has completely changed.

Form a habit of perceiving everything and everyone from the external universe that empowers you as a treasure. Everything that has a place in your life is a gift; your job is to let that gift serve you. Your job to perceive such things as treasures. They are all around you. Treasures are not scarce. Rather, they are hidden. Your job is to find them.

The moment I perceived those around me as treasures, I was able to benefit from their powers.

The moment I perceived my experiences as treasures was the moment they were able to transform me.

The moment I perceived my surroundings, my seemingly man-made problems, as *treasures* was the moment I began to realize that it was foolish to complain.

Everything is what you make it.

New York Times bestselling author, Harvard professor, and positive psychology advocate Shawn Achor explains this phenomenon in his revolutionary take on the relationship between happiness and productivity in *The Happiness Advantage*: "The simple change in mindset—i.e. a belief that [you] are taking an actual drug—is powerful enough to make the objective symptom actually disappear," or simply, change your reality.[11]

---

11   **Achor, Shawn.** The **Happiness Advantage**: The Seven Principles of Positive Psychology That Fuel Success and Performance At Work. New York: Crown Business, 2010.

You are able to morph your situation into the best possible situation, and you will enjoy it tenfold.

What's the point of making yourself miserable when you can enjoy everything life throws at you, no matter how troublesome it may seem?

Every new chapter is followed by a thrill, some type of excitement that cannot be shut down, an excitement that is seemingly inevitable. Every first is exciting; for example, opening up a gift, nagging at the wrapping paper as you reveal the treasure hiding inside that very box, waiting patiently as your family surrounds you to catch your reaction; finding out you have been accepted to your dream job, and your first day of work is the next morning; finalizing your academic schedule of classes and waiting patiently the night before your very first lecture.

Your third week of lecture is typically not as exciting as the first.

Your third day at work is typically not as exciting as the first.

Opening your tenth Christmas gift is not as exciting as opening the first.

Seeing your friend for the fourth time this week is typically not as exciting as seeing them for the first time in months.

***

The end of my fall quarter at UCLA is coming to an end, and I am dreading attending lecture. I am tired, over-worked, and the last thing I want to do is walk twenty-five minutes to one of the farthest lecture halls on campus. I skip lecture.

The decision to skip lecture as a result of my fatigue is rather *adaptation* in disguise. I lost sight of the value of lecture above merely getting participation points. I forgot that my education is a privilege, forgot the privilege of learning from an extremely accomplished professor an environment bound by learning and curiosity.

In return, *we value what is scarce to us.* We value what is not as available. We value what is limited. What is readily available, what is right in front of us, is harder to value than what is not. For if every person we knew, every object we held, and every place we traveled to was marked with a number that represented the number of times we have *left* that very person, object, or place, we would be far more grateful. We would be more attentive. We would feel an urge to be present because we know our time is no longer unlimited. We feel an urge because there is a newfound essence of scarcity.

Celebrity merchandise which is marketed under a limited edition label sparks more attention from consumers than would a product line which is available year-round.

Subsequently, we value what has a greater cost, what has a seemingly greater external value. A more expensive water bottle will be taken care of better than one you received for free. A vintage, one-of-a-kind gift will be taken care of better than something available for purchase at every store.

What is special has value; what is new has value; what is limited has value. Then, we adapt. We must instill this value no matter the external value attached to that very item, person, or experience. We can reach this through gratitude.

> *We can resist the urge to adapt through gratitude.*

This is due to the human tendency to adapt. We must resist this tendency and form a ridiculously strong habit for gratitude, for only then will we be ever so aware of our state of being, joy, and presence. We will finally realize how wonderful life truly is. We will finally realize *all is well*. Because the truth is, all is well. All is well.

> *Because the truth is, all is well.*

Likewise, the moment something is taken away is no longer available to us, *we want it*. We want it more than we ever did before when it was right in front of us. Why should we need this type of awakening to realize what we appreciate? What we have taken for granted? The value of the people we are surrounded by? The value of the meal we are eating? The value of the experience we are experiencing? We must force ourselves to build a habit to *see the incredible value that everything has! We must give gratitude on a constant basis!*

Gratitude should not be a separate practice. Gratitude is a mindset; it is a result of a newfound perspective. Your perspective is not something you unleash only five minutes out of your day; your perspective is with you everywhere you go. Your perspective is who you ARE. Your perspective is your REALITY. Thus, your GRATITUDE is your REALITY.

Your gratitude is your reality.

Let your gratitude guide you into a life filled with awe, magic, and appreciation. You will begin to see the light everywhere you go—the hidden beauty of the world, the hidden beauty of yourself and of those around you. You will no longer need any sort of awakening or moment of disturbance to realize what is important to you. You will not need a moment of loss in order to realize what you have. Rather, you will be constantly aware through newly adjusted perspectives. In turn, you will be present, aligned, and empowered every single moment of every single day. You will be unstoppable. You will have opened up your mind to possibilities which did not exist before.

"Gratitude can transform common days into thanksgivings, turn routine jobs into joy, and change ordinary opportunities into blessings."

—WILLIAM ARTHUR WARD

GETTING INTO THE HABIT OF GRATITUDE

I am so grateful. I wake up each morning to the sound of an extremely loud, hungry, barking dog, two brothers fighting to what seems to be the death of them, parents infuriated at both the barking dog and fighting brothers, and an alarm clock that decided not to go off for my morning class.

I finally get out of bed because of my craving for coffee just to see we've run out of Keurig Starbucks French Roast pods, and instant coffee, which I wouldn't dare go near, is the only thing left.

I sit in traffic almost every day and deal with drivers who want to strangle each other at the infamous intersection of Beverly Glen and Sunset.

I struggle to fit into the merging lane for the 405 North Entrance on my way back from an interview that went oh-so-poorly, almost getting hit by a truck trying to merge.

I finally get home to find my mom mad at me for how messy my room is. I want to explode because I'm already exhausted, and now I have to hear one more thing, the last thing I want to hear: My room needs to be cleaned.

I go on my computer to see it's dead.

Wow, am I grateful.

I argue with my parents over concepts that our generational gap will never allow to be understood, day and night, each time without a resolution, yet continuing to pick apart the same issues, over and over again. I try and try to explain how tradition was something of the past, and how 2019 is different from the lives they lived years ago in the heat of Tehran, Iran.

Gratitude is the answer to almost all of our problems.

We might find it convenient to make every little first-world problem described in these past five pages the biggest inconvenience, the worst thing that could ever happen to me.... but why? Why sit in anger, frustration, and annoyance over what is entirely irrelevant, and what we are luckier than ever to experience?

Gratitude is bliss.

I am so grateful I have a dog that barks and jumps all over me when I am absolutely exhausted.

I am so grateful my brothers fight day and night for they have energy and love.

I am so grateful my parents get angry because they are present and caring.

I am so grateful.

Someone snatched your parking spot? You are grateful enough to have woken up this morning, gotten ready, to have gas in your car, and to have driven all the way to that spot without an accident. I am sorry someone took your spot, but *who cares?*

Your coffee spilled all over your favorite shirt? You are grateful enough you had coffee available to you in the first place. *Who cares?*

You slept through your alarm? You are grateful enough to have woken up this morning in good health. *Who cares?*

Your turn.

Take everything you experience and write down *how grateful you are to be experiencing that thing. Each and every thing. Everyone you speak to every single day. Every place you go. Every item you possess. Every mundane activity ... transform it into the breathtaking experience it truly is.*

Your perspective is your biggest power.

Take control of how you see the world. Take control of what may initially be a problem to you, but is in actuality a blessing.... Your life will become a stream of magical events, for with everything you experience, you will understand how grateful you are to experience that thing rather than convincing yourself that everything *sucks.*

The saying, "Don't worry, be happy," is flawed. Rather, take a concrete step toward feeling ease and peace: **Preach, "Don't worry, seek gratitude."**

Don't Worry,
Seek Gratitude.

For every action, there is some sort of reaction. Yet the *magnitude* of that reaction, its strength, is determined by *you*. No one else, nothing else. In physics, we learn every action has an *equal and opposite* reaction through Newton's third law. Here, we morph this universal law into our minds by *constructing our own reactions*. No one has power over you like you may think they do. NO one. The moment you feel a loss of power, the moment someone is *provoking* a sense of false spirit out of you, remind yourself to be *nonreactive*. Remind yourself to be in tune with yourself and your surroundings, and to *remain grounded,* for that is your power.

"Non-reactivity is your superpower."

—NATASHA ADAMO

I used to let any inconvenience, surprise, or false expectation have power over me. In turn, I was left overthinking, hurt, questioning, and falling for the ultimate victim card. I micro-analyzed every action and decision I made and questioned *why* I even made that decision in the first place. I questioned my entire being, concluding I was not good enough, I should've said something different, concluding I had been largely impacted by what, in reality, was a very insignificant moment. I let *nothing* become *everything.* It was all in my head. The solution rests in being nonreactive. How can we reach this state of mind? We can accomplish this by understanding almost everything we experience is extremely insignificant; nothing matters until you make it matter. It's all up to YOU. IT'S ALL IN YOUR HEAD. I introduce the Habit of Notable Insignificance.

THE HABIT OF NOTABLE INSIGNIFICANCE

Just as we budget our spending on day-to-day purchases, we must budget our energy. Our energy is like a currency, but of much higher importance. Our energy is *everything*. *Everything is energy. Life is just energy.*

No one has it easy; everyone is *trying*. As simple as some of us are able to make life seem, *we are all on the same boat*. Simply because the girl sitting next to you at Starbucks is cruising on her phone while you frantically cram for a huge exam doesn't mean she goes to bed every night with ease. Simply because your coworker always seems to be in the best mood doesn't mean she's not struggling day and night to get food on the table.

Each of us has things to worry about. Yet our job is to let our worries coexist with the wonders of life; we must not let life's inconveniences, struggles, and more difficult moments have power over what is wonderful. We must be ever-so-aware of what may be perceived as a limitation, but not give it the power to limit us. The solution rests in how we prioritize our energy, by understanding *some things just don't matter*.

> *We have to prioritize our energy. Some things just don't matter.*

I used to let any minor inconvenience, surprise or false expectation have power over how I felt, my outlook, my state of being.... In turn, I was left overthinking, hurt, questioning, and falling for the ultimate victim card. I micro-analyzed every action and decision I made and questioned *why* I even made that decision in the first place. I questioned my entire being ...

It took too long to realize *none of this matters. Frankly, nothing matters as much as we think it does. Everything is because we make it. Life is what you make it. Take away your energy and attention from things that do not deserve to have your energy and attention!*

Understand YOUR self-worth. YOU are a commodity. You are an extremely VALUABLE commodity. You should not spare the gift of YOU on merely anyone or anything. You must be selective. You must take care of yourself. Just as celebrity guest appearances have extremely high values, YOU are no different. Protect your worth and being; do not give yourself where you are not valued or appreciated.

Ninety percent of what we give extreme power to in our lives is notably insignificant. We must build a habit to recognize what is notably insignificant and remove our energy and attention from that medium.

> *We must build a habit to recognize what is notably insignificant and remove our energy and attention from that medium.*

We have to prioritize what is deserving of our time and attention and what is not. We have to evaluate *where* we are allocating our time and *why*. We have to determine *what* we value in life, and if we are giving it the time it deserves. Why grow tired and frustrated over things that just don't matter?

First, we must determine *what* exactly matters to us and *who* matters to us, and our job to set that straight. We have to come to terms with our lives with regard to *what* we actually care about. What is most important for you to make time for? Who is most important? Why? Ask yourself. Figure it out. And then set time for those things accordingly. Less complaining, more maximizing what is truly valuable to us, what will push us forward, what we are grateful for, and what we want to accomplish.

For example, I value my friends, family, health, and academics. It took me a while to realize that. I would stay up late on Instagram instead of pampering myself with well-deserved rest. I didn't yet realize that I don't value late hours of scrolling, but instead value health and mental clarity. I would spend hours in the library struggling to understand a problem while scarfing down a bag of chips, forgetting how important my health is to me, forgetting the power of time management in preparing for exams. Where were my priorities? Clouded. I then made clear to myself what mattered most to me in life, and anything that didn't lie align with my goals was automatically filtered out. I am able to only focus on what matters, and every other little thing was wiped out. *And it felt so good.* My job is to know when my energy is being wasted and to **stop** wasting it.

Your energy is your currency. You wouldn't spend it on things you don't care for. So why treat your precious mental space any differently? Spend your time accordingly. Look at the world. Look at how huge it is and how many things are going on for every single person on that map. A lot of the problems we feel so stressed out about are entirely **insignificant.** Stop letting them take up all of your energy. Stop wasting your money.

"Character is simply habit long continued."

—PLUTARCH

ELIMINATING POOR HABITS OF THE BODY

We will now dive into the habits of the body, where we will analyze which habits do not serve us and how to minimize their impact. In order to do such, you must reevaluate what they are, determine if they set you back or set you apart, if they push you toward or away from your central mission, and which new ones must be incorporated to guide you toward the absolute best version of yourself.

I used to wake up each morning to nearly fifteen minutes of mindless scrolling on my phone. After waking up from hours of peaceful rest, the first stimulus my mind was exposed to came from some device. My mind was thrown into some sort of connectivity. My peace was disturbed the moment I woke up.

Once I got out of bed, my mind was already reacting to the stimuli coming from my phone: text messages I had missed, notifications from social media sites, news updates that flooded my home screen.... My peace was stripped the instant I turned off my alarm. I was disturbed the moment I woke up.

This habit of checking my phone was disturbing my peace. This habit was not setting me apart, but rather wasting my time, making me question my self-worth and decisions, and was not aligned with my central mission. This habit had to be broken. Yet it was one that I felt was impossible to break. I was addicted; going back was not an option.

I felt I needed my phone to wake up my mind and get me out of bed in the first place. I didn't know what else could fill that need.

I questioned *what* resource my phone provided me with: energy. The stimuli, the bright screen and stream of notifications, woke up my mind. Energy was the resource. Then, I asked, *where else can I get this resource?*

Similar to finding out your favorite makeup company tests on animals, something you don't stand by, and in turn trying to find a cruelty-free brand, your bad habit provides you with *some* return, some resource. Find out where else you can get that resource, just as you would find another make-up brand to become a customer of.

Your habits are what will push you forward into a life in which your central mission is creating the life you were born to live. Your habits can set you back or propel you forward like you never thought possible. Your habits are your secret weapon.

ASK YOURSELF, WHERE ELSE CAN I GET THIS RESOURCE?
Line up your habits. Every single one. Ask yourself, what does this habit provide me with? Then, does this habit protect my peace, does it push me forward? If not, what do I receive from this habit, and where else can I get this resource in a way where I am protected and can grow?

The Habit	Its Resource	Does It Protect My Peace and Allow Me to Grow?	If Not, Where Else Can I Get This Resource?

TAKE CONTROL OF
YOUR HABITS

THE HABITS

Here, list the habits you will begin to incorporate into your everyday life. Make sure they are extremely specific to YOU and YOUR needs.

AFFIRMATIONS

I...

CHECK INS & ADJUSTMENTS

What is working and what isn't? How do you feel? What adjustments can you make? Do you feel more liberated? Evaluate. Edit your story as much as you want. After all, this story is yours.

TAKE CONTROL OF YOUR ENERGY & ATTENTION

—

I was sitting at the library a week before what I anticipated to be an extremely difficult, demanding exam. My laptop was fully charged, my coffee was hot and sweetened, my pens had ink and my notebooks were open. I was ready to tackle the beast of organic chemistry.

I had everything I needed in order to study effectively, I thought. My materials were carefully packed into my backpack and placed onto my desk at my favorite library. I reviewed the material the night before so I was in the correct mindset to study the day after. I was ready.

A week before, I was experiencing the most stress I had ever experienced as I prepared to launch my book for pre-sale. I was all over the place to say the least.

My thoughts from the week before did not remain in the week before; they were constantly circulating in my mind, especially in the moments when I needed to forget about the book altogether—moments such as frantically preparing for what I expected to be an extremely difficult exam. I couldn't focus. I kept thinking about the book. Yes, this book.

What was the issue at hand? My attention.

I sat and continued to question why I couldn't focus, why I was thinking about something that had *nothing* to do with the matter at hand: organic chemistry. Finally, I questioned myself about *where* my attention was in comparison to where it *needed* to be. This one question, which was asked with no intention of leading to any possible solution, shifted my focus and changed *everything*.

I took out a pen and paper in order to organize my thoughts as I formulated a response. My attention was on a project that induced stress and fear: my book launch. Although beyond exciting in every regard, it was *stressful*. Extremely.

And it was constantly on my mind.

So, I forced myself to *redirect my attention*.

This simple example from an academic setting—studying for an organic chemistry class—proves the power of attention in the most complex realms of our everyday life. Attention is everything. Our attention makes up who we are.[12]

---

12 Gallagher, Winifred. Rapt: Attention and the Focused Life. Penguin, 2009.

In times of distress, redirect your attention.

What we focus on—where our attention lies—is what grows in our lives. What we think more about, talk more about, direct more attention to, is what grows.

We become what we think about. Energy flows where attention goes.

—RHONDA BYRNE

We need to direct our attention toward what allows us to grow, to experience peace and happiness. But how do we do that? First, we must evaluate what is good for us: what our body wants more of, and what our body wants less of. Then, we have to find out where we can get what's good for us, and where we can get rid of what's bad for us. Then, go crazy. Saturate yourself with those things—with those treasures. Make them your life. Throw away the trash. Let's say someone placed a giant bucket in front of you filled with diamonds and crushed soda cans. Imagine that. Both are evenly mixed throughout. The bucket has a note that says, "You can take three items from this bucket." So, you begin to scan the bucket. You see the mixture of beautiful, dazzling diamonds along with what initially confuses you: soda cans. What?

What would you do? It doesn't require much thought; you'd pick out three diamonds. Why would you pick three crushed soda cans? Your attention subconsciously directed you to the *good*. It has been engraved in us that diamonds are good and that trash is bad. So, we must engrave in our minds what is good for us and what is bad so it becomes *that* simple—as simple as picking out diamonds from a pile of trash—to direct our attention to the right people, experiences, places, and things.

Social media is the bad to me. I really dislike it. I only like it when it's used properly. I define the appropriate use of social media as using it to inspire, communicate, share light, and spread knowledge. If I am using it for those narrowly defined purposes, then I feel fulfilled with the time I've spent on it. If I am using it to compare myself to others and their experiences, I feel great regret once my scrolling time is up. So, what have I done about that? I have redirected my attention from social media. This means using it extremely sparingly. This means only opening the app with the mindset that I will either use it to learn something, to communicate something, to share light, or to inspire.

Reading is the good to me. I love reading. It fills me with knowledge and inspiration. It grounds me. It makes me feel centered and focused. So, what have I done? I read so much! I have made it one of the biggest centers of attention in my life—it has become so large in my mind that I am filled with all of its side effects: knowledge, inspiration, feeling centered … how powerful is that? My family is also a form of good to me. So, I make time to spend time with them. I am sure to be off my phone and to be present. I focus so much on my family—where my attention is exclusively on them—that they become larger and larger in my mind, and I reap the benefits of spending that time with them. I feel fulfilled, I feel loved, I feel happy.

We can break our lives into several chunks. Each of these chunks takes up a certain amount of our attention, time, and energy. Each chunk requires adequate attention, time, and energy in order to grow and blossom. Yet each chunk—each area of our lives—is deprived of this case once fear enters the equation. And that stops it from growing.

In turn, that stops *you* from growing. A seed cannot grow into a sunflower if its owner forgets to water it. That's it. Your chunks are your seeds, your mind is the owner, and your attention, time, and energy are the water.

We can separate life's chunks by using Zig Ziglar's Wheel of Life: a very strong approach to life balance and goal setting.[13]

- Physical/Health
- Personal and Social Circle
- Work and Career
- Family
- Spiritual
- Financial
- Mind/Intellect

Your Health: Do you have a healthy lifestyle—regular exercise, eat healthy—to live as long as you can?

Your Personal Life and Social Life: This includes who you spend your time with as well as the things you spend your personal time doing.

---

13   Ziglar Inc. "Ziglar Inc - The Wheel of Life," November 11, 2016. https://www.ziglar.com/articles/the-wheel-of-life/.

Your Work Life: Are you where you would like to be in your work or career?

Your Family Life: Do you spend time nurturing your family relationships?

Your Spiritual Life: Do you make time to study and grow spiritually?

Your Money: How well are you doing to meet your monthly and yearly budget? Are you saving? Investing?

Your Mind/Intellect: Do you read books, do crossword puzzles, learn new things, study to improve your knowledge, develop yourself personally, and keep your mind strong?

Ask yourself what demands more and less of your attention and energy from this wheel. Are you devoting too much energy and attention towards your work life and not enough to your personal and social life? Are you neglecting the need for a monthly budget, in turn costing your personal and social life?

TAKE CONTROL OF YOUR ENERGY AND ATTENTION

REDIRECTION

Here, write what you want to devote more, less, and no energy/attention to.

MORE:

LESS:

NONE:

AFFIRMATIONS

I give more attention to...

because...

I give less attention to...

because...

I do not give any attention to...

because...

CHECK INS & ADJUSTMENTS

What is working and what isn't? How do you feel? What adjustments can you make? Do you feel more liberated? Evaluate. Edit your story as much as you want. After all, this story is yours.

TAKE CONTROL OF YOUR ENVIRONMENT

—

ENVIRONMENT TRUMPS MOTIVATION

In *Atomic Habits,* a *New York Times* bestselling book, author James Clear discusses the power of environment over motivation, and how environment nearly trumps it completely.[14] Your self-motivation is not enough. Your environment must be in tune with what you are trying to accomplish. Let your environment move you forward, not detract from your central mission.

Just as you must surround yourself with people who support you, you must place yourself in an environment that *supports you,* that supports your mission, that is in tune with *what you want to accomplish.*

---

14   Clear, James. Atomic Habits: Tiny Changes, Remarkable Results : An Easy & Proven Way to Build Good Habits & Break Bad Ones. New York: Avery, an imprint of Penguin Random House, 2018. Print.

Let your environment move you forward, not detract from your central mission.

Coffee shops place the tip jar near the register so when customers receive change, they can toss some in the jar if they decide to. Leaving the tip jar at the opposite end of the coffee shop, where no one would be likely to see it or think to leave change behind, would be foolish. They are taking advantage of their environment in order to maximize sales.

What is accessible and convenient is what is gravitated toward. As Clear explains in *Atomic Habits*, you should design your environment so it sets you up for success. Make your life easier.

Design your environment so that it sets you up for success. Make your life easier.

HelloFresh, a meal kit delivery service, filled the niche of at-home cooking by delivering the exact ingredients, portions, and directions needed to cook a complete meal in convenient packages to the consumer's home. This takes out all the time-consuming preparation that would ordinarily steer people away from taking on at-home cooking. Everything is already prepared for them. HelloFresh is marketing convenience. Someone might be inspired yet reluctant to start cooking more, but once the ingredients are right in front of them, the task becomes much less of a burden and, in turn, is easier to complete.

Preparing your lunch the night before forces you to bring a home-prepped meal to school or work instead of purchasing your lunch that day. It's waiting for you in the fridge. It has been conveniently prepared for you. It drives the action of *not* purchasing lunch.

Convenience drives action.
Force convenience.

Figure out what you need to do and then design your environment accordingly. Make your environment a place where the actions you want to take are convenient enough to pursue. Be smart and specific, noting that *everyone's needs vary.* Some people enjoy loud, upbeat spaces for getting work done where others need silence. Some find peace on a hike where others are moved by the ocean. Determine what you need and how your environment will help you obtain that. Maximize your space; let it move you forward.

When I Need	This Is Where I Will Go
To Focus	
To Work	
To Create	
To Think	
To Energize	
To Breathe	
To Rest	
To Question	

"You are a product of your environment. So choose the environment that will best develop you toward your objective. Analyze your life in terms of its environment. Are the things around you helping you toward success—or are they holding you back?"

—W. CLEMENT STONE

TAKE CONTROL OF
YOUR DEVICES

———

Our devices are gadgets we've convinced ourselves only function in our favor, gadgets that make life easier, bring convenience to another level, and let us connect like never before.

And yes, these devices *have* changed our lives! They *do* provide such services. Being able to call an Uber to take you from A to B in a matter of seconds or seeing the face a loved one thousands of miles away through Facetime *is* truly revolutionary. But when does it get dangerous? When do our gadgets begin to do more harm than we ever thought possible? When are they no longer functioning in our favor? When are they *destructive*?

When they have taken control over our lives … when our productive, focused moments turn into hours of distraction and then transform into stress … when our plans to be social turn into merely staring at our screens. How outrageous! These little devices, these screens, have made us *slaves* to their use! We are humans, nearly the most brilliant species to have ever lived with some of the most *insane* capabilities, yet we have fallen for the trap of screen addiction, and *very few people* have succeeded in freeing themselves from it. The time has come for us to experience freedom: digital freedom.[15]

Why is this relevant to finally creating the life you so immensely desire? Or if you just want to find new ways to make your life *that* much better? Because once we experience freedom—in whatever regard it may be—**we experience control**, and an extremely prevalent ingredient in this equation is yes, digital freedom. We can finally spend time how *we* want to spend it. We are able to *focus* better. We are able to do everything we want to do because we are free, we are focused.

> *Focus is power. Unleash your power to focus.*
> *Free yourself from the screen.*

In *Digital Minimalism*, Cal Newport uses the analogy of a cost-benefit analysis when using our phones and social networking sites in order to further understand *what* we are sacrificing for the so-called benefits that come from our phones.

***

It's as if we have no room to think in isolation because all of our time is spent responding to what's on the screen.

---

15 Newport, Cal. Digital Minimalism: Choosing a Focused Life in a Noisy World. Penguin, 2019.

Whether it be an incoming text message, Snapchat notification, or your daily Twitter feed, our devices have taken control over us. **We've become slaves to what is not even real.** We have become nearly obedient to our devices; this obsession is the most pressing epidemic the human race is facing, yet has no solution is being mapped for it. We are sitting in ignorance to an utter plague, the **plague of the media**, I call it. The time has come to take control. We must optimize how we use our devices for any other passive use is *in turn controlling us without us even realizing it.* And what a waste of time! A complete waste of time!

Trying so hard to stay connected *all the time* is completely *disconnecting* us from one another. Checking every single app, scrolling through every single feed, watching every single story, responding to every single incoming message has become part of our routine ... This is **hyper-connectivity!** Humans are not meant to be hyper-connected.

In turn, we become *drained* by the amount of energy we've put into keeping up socially *online* and engaging with each other in real life becomes both a burden and *difficult!* We are not used to it! This is terrifying.

And why is this the case? Why have we become so addicted so quickly? We are feeding right into what these networks want: **an online addiction.** They want us to be addicted to their services, so every little widget that all of these applications have are there for the sole purpose of making us use the service for longer and longer periods of time. Snapchat streaks? They convince users they have created some sort of strong relationship by having a longer streak; in reality, users are sending meaningless images to each other every single day with no underlying purpose. Snapchat, in turn, is persuading users to use the app, well, *every single day*. They have succeeded. *How does that make you feel?*

You might argue, why? Social media has *so many benefits!* It allows us to grow our network, connect to more people than ever, catch up with friends and, of course, stay connected! Why take control of something so valuable?

When used appropriately, *of course it is valuable.* Social media has the power to *empower* just as it has the power to destroy. Its destruction lies in its two major abilities:

TIME WASTING AND MOOD CRUSHING.
I've divided all the evil powers of social media into two categories: its ability to waste your time and crush your mood. Let's dive a little deeper.

Social media is a time waster. It throws you into a time warp where minutes turn into hours and drives you to forget what you opened that very application for in the first place. What does this mean? It robs you of your time without you even realizing it. Social media is a *master* thief. It takes away what you didn't realize you ever owned in the first place: time.

"I have no time!"
"I'm so busy!"
"I'm just so backed up!"

False. You have time. Your time checking Instagram or responding to a Snapchat adds up *ridiculously fast.* The result? You are less productive. You don't get as much done. You are distracted. You run out of time.

You also become *low on energy.* Staying updated all day through your phone is *draining* you without you even realizing it. In turn, sure, you might have time to make plans with friends and family, but you don't have the *energy* for those plans anymore. You are socially drained from the least social device of all: your phone

Guess what else it does! Drives you into the world of toxic **social comparison**! It's a one-way ticket to feeling inferior and inadequate, a one-way ticket to misery. **It is a mood crusher.**

We have grown accustomed to capturing moments and instilling some desire to *share* that moment. For some reason, other people should know what we are up to.... How foolish is this idea once thought about? **Sharing our lives is an incredible privilege. Share later. Be present now.**

Take photos. Film yourself. Film your loved ones. Transform them into beautiful movies you can watch later. Print out the photos and look at them whenever the desire strikes. Extract your life from the screen. Bring your memories to *life* instead of keeping them imprisoned in some *device.*

Try it for yourself. Force yourself to *live in the moment* while also *capturing memories.* Yes, you can do both! Photos are a beautiful thing. Videos are a beautiful thing. Memories are a beautiful thing. Keep them. Hold onto them. But please, *bring them to life.*

And so, how do we break free of this addiction? How do we take back control of something that is slipping away by the second, something that we can never get back, our time?

In order to go full force into optimizing our desires, in order to bring them to life, we must take control of what we can control, one of those being **our relationship to the screen**: social media sites, applications, emails, etc. We can do this concretely in three steps. However, we must be dedicated, focused, and persistent.

You must constantly remind yourself of your end goal and the steps you are going to take to achieve that goal. Do not grow forgetful. Do not put it aside for a moment because it will slip away, and the end result will be that much farther away …

So, what's the solution? How do you take control of your devices? Here are three concrete steps you can take to take control of what was once yours, as advised by Newport.[16]

1. SCHEDULE YOUR SOCIAL MEDIA TIME STRICTLY.

Just as you schedule time for meetings and time with friends, schedule your social media time. Tell yourself you are only free to scroll between the times of 6:00 p.m. and 6:15 p.m.

---

16 Newport, Cal. Digital Minimalism: Choosing a Focused Life in a Noisy World. Penguin, 2019.

every day. You have no time outside of that time frame. My scrolling time is between 6 p.m. and 6:30 p.m. every day. I let myself go on Instagram every day because I am currently doing marketing for this very book, so it is my *work* time in addition to my leisure.

2. BE EXTREMELY PURPOSEFUL WITH YOUR USAGE.

Ask yourself why you are using the app in the first place. If you are mindlessly scrolling, admit to it. If you are looking for some sort of inspiration, confirm that. If you are trying to be informed on a topic, determine the topic before you dive into the heap of posts among posts.

3. REMOVE APPLICATIONS THAT SERVE NO BENEFIT TO YOUR LIFE.

If your relationship with someone was not strengthened after having them on some social media platform, either stop using that application or reinvent how you use that application. I discovered having Snapchat streaks did not strengthen a single one of my relationships. The action of having a streak convinced me that I was connecting to people, but rather, I was sending them one photo each day with little meaning. That is the weakest form of connection.

TAKE CONTROL OF
YOUR DEVICES

RULES

Here, create a set of rules you will abide by in regards to your devices.

AFFIRMATIONS
I...

CHECK INS & ADJUSTMENTS

What is working and what isn't? How do you feel? What adjustments can you make? Do you feel more liberated? Evaluate. Edit your story as much as you want. After all, this story is yours.

TAKE CONTROL OF
YOUR BOUNDARIES

———

How are you supposed to make your grandma's special brownies, which require a very special recipe, if someone keeps adding extra flour into the mix when the recipe strictly called for two-and-a-half cups of all-purpose flour?

You can't. Grandma's special brownies require a special recipe that needs to be followed. If that recipe is tinkered with, well, they won't be made as they are supposed to be.

Your plans, dreams, and the best version of yourself are the equivalent to grandma's special brownies. If your specific recipe is tinkered with by others, how are you supposed to get to your final destination, the extraordinary?

Our flow state is the mental and physical state where we finally feel in control. There, we have acquired some sort of rhythm, are in tune with our decisions, and are free. There, we are stable, strong, resilient, fearless, passionate, filled with gratitude and at peace with ourselves. You may have not reached your flow state yet. But, once you have taken control of all of the elements we have just discussed, protecting the state you have worked tirelessly to reach is vital. You must protect your flow state at all costs. You can do this through boundary-setting.

> *Discover your flow state and protect it at all costs.*

Boundary-setting allows us to carefully filter out who is allowed to enter the grand home we have spent the last 150 pages building. Boundary-setting allows us to tune into our desires and our purpose and simply filter out whatever does not line up with our desires and our purpose.

"I allow myself to set healthy boundaries. To say no to what does not align with my values, to say yes to what does. Boundaries assist me to remain healthy, honest and living a life that is true to me."

—LEE HORBACHEWSKI

TAKE CONTROL OF
YOUR BOUNDARIES

THE BOUNDARIES

Here, create a list of boundaries you want to define for yourself. Brainstorm. Where do you feel you have lost control that you would like to take back?

AFFIRMATIONS

I...

CHECK INS & ADJUSTMENTS

How are your newly formed boundaries serving you? What is working and what isn't? How do you feel? What adjustments can you make? Do you feel more liberated? Evaluate. Edit your story as much as you want. After all, this story is yours.

THE POWER OF EXCELLENT EXECUTION

———

Now, *how* will we create these habits? How will we make them so strong they are nearly impossible to break? Through the power of executing your goals with excellence. I introduce The Power of Excellent Execution.

John Doerr, former computer engineer and current venture capitalist, stands by the power of setting the right goals and how to execute them in the ability to foster the most pressing forms of change.[17]

Everything is about excellent execution, he explains, which can be understood in terms of a simple acronym, OKRs, which stand for objectives and key results. The two elements have a clear link, a fairly direct cause-and-effect relationship.

---

17   Doerr, John. 'Why the Secret to Success Is Setting the Right Goals.' https://www.ted.com/talks/john_doerr_why_the_secret_to_success_ is_setting_the_right_goals/transcript.

How you set yourself up for success is what dictates your results. Here, your objectives are your how. *What* are you trying to achieve? *How* are you going to get there? These objectives can be then translated to a succinct, effective form of goal setting. Your success—your results—are your key results. These come as a result of *how* you set yourself up for what you want to achieve through your goals. These are not just any goals. You must be specific, reasonable, and strict.

This method can be seen in business organizations who are *constantly* setting objectives for their teams. Different organizations have different weekly, monthly, and yearly quotas to meet, for example. This is a clear example of goal setting in the real world, where the key results are of extremely high importance. Company X might have to export millions of boxes by April where Company Z is pushing to sell out of their most newly launched product. Everyone has goals, whether they are clearly defined as goals or not.

But how do they ensure these objectives, these goals, are set the right way? How do they maximize productivity in the workplace with regard to setting the right objectives? How can you apply this strategy to your own life?

You "must answer the question, 'Why?'" Doerr explains. **Why.** Your purpose. Your primary motivation. Your reason. Simply, *why* are you doing what you are doing? Finding your purpose, understanding why you are even bothering with a certain task, is one of the strongest and most effective ways of motivating yourself, and the right form of motivation is what will lead you to that path of success, the path that grants you your key results.

"Truly transformational teams combine their ambitions to their passion and to their purpose, and they develop a clear and compelling sense of why."

—JOHN DOERR

And that is the concept exactly. That is the connection between all these terms we've been throwing around: objectives, goals, results, success, efficiency, why, purpose. Your purpose is the glue, the foundation, to any form of success you want to pursue. Your purpose guides you to where you want to be.

Imagine you want to build a house. Your friend finds out you want to build a house. They ask you, "So, what are you building this house for?" You don't have a response because you don't know your why. Your purpose is absent. Your purpose is foundational. Will the house really be built? **Purpose is your foundation.**

Now, once our foundation has been established, we connect these to our *what*, what we want to build, the blueprint of the house. Now that we know *why* we even want this house built, we must gather the materials to build it! We need our what. Our what, our objectives, must be:

- **Significant**
- **Action-oriented**
- **Inspiring**
- **Concrete**

What you want from yourself must follow those guidelines. The things you want to accomplish must be clear and exciting enough for you to have a burning desire to accomplish them. Make some goals right now. Place this book aside for a few minutes and write three long-term goals for yourself. Let's say you want these accomplished by the end of this month. Here's an example:

Example Objectives for January:

- Finish reading *Genius Foods* by January 30
- Drink sixty ounces of water every single day consistently, form habit by January 30
- Be more confident by January 30

Goal #1: Is it significant? Reading is significant and empowering, so yes. Is it action-oriented? Yes. It is telling me something to do. Is it inspiring? For sure. Is it anti-fuzzy thinking? Definitely. I find a book and read it. There's not much to it besides that.

Goal #2: Is it significant? Kind of. This is not what I'm really talking about here. This mode of excellent execution is a guideline to achieving large missions. Keep those small goals for the goal guidelines I explained in the chapter Creating Your Goal Sheet.

Goal #3: Is it significant? Yes. Is it action-oriented? Absolutely not! *How* will I be more confident by January 30th? This objective lacks the most integral element: specificity. It is not action-oriented. It is not telling me to do something. How can I reap key results without the right objectives? How can you enjoy a delicious loaf of banana bread without the right ingredients?

Let's tweak these goals a little bit....

Finish reading *Genius Foods* and explain the most important lessons of the book to a friend and Mom. *We made this goal more specific with the aspect of teaching. Teaching and spreading knowledge are powers we do not always use. Learning is a goal of its own, but teaching and spreading knowledge lies entirely complementary. The goal is measurable because we want it done by the end of the month and because a single explanation meets this objective.*

- Drink sixty ounces of water every day consistently to feel and look as hydrated and healthy as possible. *The experience of health and hydration are extremely significant.*
- *Those are significant aspects of my health. These must be clear in your objectives.*
- Work towards self-confidence by wearing clothing that make me feel most myself and asking one question in every class I attend. *Here we have established **action**, how I plan to chase after confidence. The objective is already significant. It is inspiring. There we go.*

These objectives have now been joined by our key results, which meet the following guidelines:

- **Specific and time-bound**
- **Aggressive yet realistic**
- **Measurable and verifiable**

In 1999, Doerr introduced this concept of OKRs to Google.[18] Every member of Google is instructed, to this day, to write down their objectives and key results. Google does not do this to grant the employees promotions or alter their contracts, but rather, "to get collective commitment," to truly stretch their employees beyond what they believe they are capable of.

In 2008, Sundar Pichai took on an objective: build the best browser. That's pretty significant, inspiring, and action-oriented. How did he attach this to his key results to truly accomplish this goal? Key result: twenty million users in three years. This goal was specific, aggressive, measurable, and time-bound. "Every year he stuck to those key results, but amped it up each year.... By his third year he upped the ante to 100,000,000 million, launching an effective marketing campaign and everything else. . ."[19]

He stuck to his objectives and key results consistently, and he continued to reap the results of achievement. He stuck to his why. He continued to be aggressive. He was specific with what he wanted. He knew how he was going to get it. So, he got it.

---

18   "When John Doerr Brought a 'Gift' to Google's Founders." *Wired*. https://www.wired.com/story/when-john-doerr-brought-a-gift-to-googles-founders/.

19   Doerr, John. 'Why the Secret to Success Is Setting the Right Goals.' https://www.ted.com/talks/john_doerr_why_the_secret_to_success_is_setting_the_right_goals/transcript.

CREATING YOUR SUPERHERO

Now that we've addressed *what you want* in the form of your burning desires, come to terms with *how* your story would change if you were fearless; we must manifest this vision. A dream is only a dream until it is manifested so deeply it can come to life. You are going to manifest this extraordinary version of yourself, one who is no longer phased by fear, welcomes failure, pushes for pure authenticity, by molding these characteristics into your **superhero**. You are going to create your superhero. Then, you will become it. The time has come to bring your vision to life.

As a child, a superhero was the ultimate idol. Why do children love superheroes?

Superheroes give kids a sense of **control** and **power** they would otherwise deem nonexistent. They are able to accomplish the impossible, such as saving the world or fighting off bad guys. They are empowering.[20]

We must channel this exact sense of **control** and **power** that superheroes exhibit. The mind is where these powers rest. We do not need to know how to fly at the speed of light or have superhuman strength in order to have a newfound sense of control and power. Once our mind is in the state to have a profound sense of self, sense of our surroundings, sense of desire, and the ability to overcome ... we are unstoppable. Our superhero is the mind. And, funnily enough, we each have one.

A superhero is defined as a "fictional hero having extraordinary or superhuman powers." As Stan Lee explained in "What Makes a Superhero," a superhero is not perfect; they are not just one- or two-dimensional: "You want a three-dimensional superhero who lives and breathes and worries.... except for the fact that he or she has a superpower."[21]

Your superhero is not a perfect, almighty source of wisdom. Your superhero is not merely an inspirational, fictional character. Your superhero is a *hero with extraordinary powers*. You must become your own hero by unleashing your extraordinary powers. The human spirit is extraordinary.

---

20 HuffPost UK. "Why Children Love Playing Superhero," September 15, 2015. https://www.huffingtonpost.co.uk/dr-niamh/why-children-love-playing-superhero_b_8133480.html.

21 "(5) What Makes a Superhero? | Stan Lee | TEDxGateway 2013 - YouTube." Accessed January 26, 2020. https://www.youtube.com/watch?v=DSGf6i-s3U2w.

The human spirit is bountiful in its abilities. The human spirit is nearly limitless. Yet we often let ourselves settle for the ordinary. We let ourselves sit in a mindset that is comfortable, a mindset that is not challenged. In turn, growth *is* limited. We do not unlock our full potential. We must push ourselves to bring our extraordinary powers to life in order to unleash ourselves into a life truly worth living.

The free man or woman is quietly confident and peaceful. Aware of both their strengths and weaknesses, they seek self-analysis to improve themself. She is a woman of integrity; her word is better than a signed contract. His mind is constantly filled with gratitude, appreciation, and all manner of positive thoughts. She is a leader who is prepared to take the initiative. He is a man of character, self-control, and firm will. She lives by bringing happiness to other people's lives.[22]

How do you create your superhero? Where do you begin?

1. Central Mission
What is this character's central mission? What makes them feel fulfilled each and every day? What is their central purpose? What will he or she be remembered for?

2. Superpowers
What powers will help this superhero accomplish that mission? What qualities does this character exhibit?

---

22 Kelly, Matthew. The Rhythm of Life: Living Every Day with Passion and Purpose. Simon and Schuster, 2004.

3. Character Development

What is this superhero like? What are their habits? How do they spend their time? What does they like and dislike? What do they value? What do they prioritize?

4. Goals: Long Term & Short Term

What does this character want to accomplish? What are their goals?

5. Final Touches

Anything else you'd like to add? What about a final costume? What do they look like? Do they stand up straight? What about the way they carry themselves? What about this person makes them *feel* extraordinary?

Central Mission	Superpowers	Character	Goals	Final Touches

Now, present your superhero as if you are pitching them to a television show. Describe every single detail, down to the smallest character flaws. This superhero is not perfect, but who they are will allow them to live an extraordinary life.

Now, get visual. Draw your superhero, noting each and every building block you have included while creating this character.

Now, your job is to bring this character to life. You will become this superhero. You will manifest the powers you have given them by reciting out loud, into the universe, that you have already acquired the powers your superhero has.

Example: My name is Nicolette Khalifian. I am strong, independent, and inspired. I value health above all, my family, my friends, and education. I am nonreactive, patient, kind, foolish, and a dreamer.

Continue using this structure. You must speak of yourself in the present tense. Bring your superhero to life.

Recite these affirmations every single morning before you go about your day. Remind yourself of the person you have a burning desire to become. You do not deserve anything less.

BECOMING MY SUPERHERO:
POWER AFFIRMATIONS

PART THREE

OPTIMIZE & RISE

Now that we have taken the necessary steps to bring our vision to life by taking control of various means, we must steer it clear of any excuses, habits, and expectations that may take us in the wrong direction. This is the equivalent to clearing the road after a large snowfall in order to ensure a smooth drive with few complications. We cannot avoid an unexpected blizzard, but we can clean off the snow that has already fallen from our driveway. We can set ourselves up for success.

You will have taken control of everything you can; you have strategized what welcomes strategy. The rest you will let flow; you will rise and allow all the pieces to come together. You will finally feel at peace.

We will replace any of these complications with understandings, habits, and complete mindset shifts that will, at last, lead us to the most balanced, peaceful, extraordinary life possible.

ADAPTATION TRAPS

Adaptations are a trap. They force us into a loss of gratitude and an episodic life. We go about our days with little to no treasure for the privileges we are given, such as simply waking up and having a cup of coffee to start our day. These are *privileges.* Yet, once we adapt, we lose sight of every privilege we have been granted. We become adapted and are not easily impressed. Rather, we fill this void, a void once filled with excitement for a new chapter and awe, with complaints. Once something falls into some regular form—whatever that might be—it loses its spark.

Our job is to keep the spark alive.

Once the spark is rekindled, excitement follows every action we take. Our lives are once again filled with purpose and meaning. We see the world from the lens we once did when we were first exposed to it.

The excitement in traveling to a new destination, the excitement in opening up your very first Christmas present ... the excitement in the *unknown* ... we must bring back this excitement into everywhere we have fallen into the trap of adaptation. We must rekindle the fire within us.

Every sunset, each and every home-cooked meal, every cup of tea, and every moment spent with family and friends must be taken with gratitude and awe. We have no reason not to... no reason to miss out on the beauties of this world simply because we are *used to them*. Unless we bring this adaptation into existence, such a phenomenon does not exist.

The moment one of these experiences, people, places, or things is stripped from us, our gratitude peaks, and we begin to regret taking any of them for granted. Our job is to bring back this fire so we never again have to regret not having a full understanding of what we once had now that it's gone.

I was trapped. I was trapped because I lacked two of the most important pillars of a fulfilling life: purpose and meaning. Rather, my purpose was understood as something meaningless, as success in the wrong mediums: success in the workplace, success in materials, success on paper. I was trapped in an episodic life in which my true purpose was fogged by what I believed I was *supposed* to have.

"For the most part, people today perceive their purpose in relation to success in the workplace and financial independence. The result is what we witness before us in our world today and what we too often allow ourselves to be a part of—a panicked frenzy of people rushing around, working too much, working too hard, working too often ..."

—MATTHEW KELLY, THE RHYTHM OF LIFE

As students, we have a set schedule that we follow for a semester. In time, we get into the swing of a routine. Class at this time, lunch at this time, study at this time, see friends at this time, office hours at that time ... and then it becomes so routine, so regular, that we grow distant from the initial excitement this very schedule brought us when we first received it.

Remember that first moment you had your finalized class schedule? The excitement and fear, the nerves, the questioning of what you're going to wear and who you're going to sit next to ... we all feel it. And then, in time, we grow **adaptive.** We have adapted to this lifestyle, to this schedule. And then the excitement begins to fade. The initial joy we had found in those first few days of classes begins to diminish.

Remember your first day of work? Ah, so exciting. A brand new place, new colleagues, new tasks, and new duties. Everything is new, everything is exciting. We are *so* excited! We prepared our outfit the night before and already planned out what we are having for lunch during our break. And then, as days go by, we get tired. We get used to it. Your desk doesn't bring the joy it did on your first day and your lunch break isn't as rewarding as it was when you first started out. The initial joy we found in the first few days of our new job begins to diminish.

We have adapted.

Routines make us too comfortable. Routines make us fall for the episodic trap. How do we stay in routine while also keeping our circumstances as exciting, fun, and fresh as possible? How do we look forward to each new day as if it is our very first? Our last? How do we hold onto that excitement for as long as we can? How do we prolong the honeymoon period? How do we *live* for each and every day to start, not checking the time periodically to see when it will finally end?

What makes the first day of school, work, or vacation all so exciting?

The excitement is rooted in the idea that it feels like a *new chapter.*

Spoiler: every single morning you wake up you are opening up a fresh page of your chapter. It is no different. We must treat every single day like it is our last—or it is our first—like it is our birthday. We are excited, scared, and *looking forward* for what the day has in store.

Being busy is the new brag-card. Oh, you work forty hours a week? I work forty-five! Oh, you're tired? I haven't slept in three days! We engage in a one-up battle with those around us because apparently being busy is being superior and taking a step back—valuing sleep, health, relaxation, and alone time—is entirely inferior, a sign of weakness and *laziness.* However, the opposite perspective still holds some truth; understanding *what* you value and how you will direct your attention to those values and priorities is the most powerful understanding one can have.

We must resist the urge to adapt. **Gratitude** resists this urge to adapt.

THE RACE TO MISERY

———

I convinced myself I had no time for anyone or anything I cared about. I convinced myself I was too busy. I became a participant in the race for misery without consenting to it. I fell into the trap. I convinced myself my workload and the new life that college entailed was simply a life that must be dedicated toward work and work only.... that free time would no longer exist.

I convinced myself *this was how it was going to be,* that this new lifestyle—where students are frantically running around overbooked, intensely stressed, and hyper-connected—was normal. Everyone was in a race to misery, and the greater your struggles, the more intense your schedule, the more chaos you experienced, the closer you were to the finish line. We all seem to be in a competition to reach some sort of expiration. We are supposed to feel fatigue, burn-out, and absolute exhaustion; free time does not exist, and having time for leisure, having time to merely be, having time to make a phone call, or watch a movie you've been wanting to see is translated as *laziness* ... to *not working hard enough.*

CHAOS IS NOT COOL

Free will seems to no longer exist, as if we have agreed to be miserable, as though overworking oneself is *expected*. Chaos is glamorized. Stress is glamorized. Peace of mind doesn't exist. This is absurdity at its finest.

1. *Chaos is not cool.*

I was once a victim of this type of mindset, in which my priorities were defective, and I was convinced I was always too busy to fit in time for *anything* I even *remotely* cared about. I was madly influenced by my environment to the point that I, indeed, felt my free will disappeared *without even realizing it*. I was submitting to a lifestyle I never agreed to. Suddenly, I saw myself sleeping five hours a night, having incredibly poor time management, running around day and night, having little to no free time, while simultaneously watching my relationships with myself and with others suffer. I was absolutely lost.

Students are on the hunt to max out their schedules due to the misunderstanding that *if you are busy, you're doing something right.* We are almost forced into this lifestyle, as if free will diminishes in the face of a greater workload.

Being immersed in a life that is chaotic, frantic, unhealthily fast-paced, and distorted is not normal. Feeling constantly tired, exhausted, and overworked is not normal. This experience is not normal. You are not meant to live this kind of life.

We must slow down. We must remove chaos from our lives every way we can. We must instill a burning desire to experience peace of mind in every way possible. We must instill a burning desire to be still, to be nonreactive, to be at one with ourselves and our surroundings. We must instill a burning desire to be serene and tranquil and welcome feelings of solitude.

How is this possible amidst a busy life? How is this possible amidst an array of responsibilities which we feel we have no control over? How is it possible if we are constantly running around and feel as though we have no way around it? No solution comes overnight, but we can dive deep into self-inquiry to see *how* we spend our time, determine if we are allocating time to what we *truly value*, *re-evaluate* our priorities and, in turn, *make adjustments* as needed.

1. Write out your entire schedule and determine how you spend your time. Every hour of every day—what do they go toward? Be honest with yourself. What is your schedule so terribly backed up with? Of those responsibilities, which do you value and which do you feel forced into? Write out your entire schedule, from morning to when you go to bed. Take note of *where you are wasting your time.* Do you spend more than an hour on your phone each day? Do you waste time on Instagram when you could be meeting a friend who you said you were too busy to make time for? Of the responsibilities you don't value, **why are they on your schedule?**

2. Write down your priorities. What do you prioritize? Who do you prioritize?

Are you allocating the right number of hours to these priorities? Do these priorities appear on your schedule?

3. Hit delete. Remove what is *wasting your time*, what you *don't value*, and what is simply being *inefficient*. Hit delete.

4. Plug your priorities back into your schedule. Replace what you don't prioritize with the things you actually do.

5. Create your Free Block. Pick a time block to do whatever you want. This time block can never be touched; no one can interfere with your Free Block. Treat it like an extra class or meeting; it is booked every single day, and it can never be moved. I have a free block every single day from 6 p.m. to 7 p.m. During this time, I can do whatever I want in that moment. I don't plan my free block. If I want to call a friend, I can do so during this time period. If I want to watch a new YouTube video, I can do so. If I want to meet up with a friend to quickly catch up, I can do so during my free block.

6. Fill in the empty spaces with your *leisure*. This could be making time for learning a new instrument, playing a sport, or meeting up with a friend. Your leisure should appear *whenever you have a freed-up schedule. You must have free time every single day. You must make time for leisure every single day.*

1. *Write out your entire schedule.*

Time	How Are You Spending It?
8:00 a.m.–9:00 a.m.	
9:00 a.m.–10:00 a.m.	
10:00 a.m.–11:00 a.m.	
11:00 a.m.–12:00 p.m.	
12:00 p.m.–1:00 p.m.	
1:00 p.m.–2:00 p.m.	
2:00 p.m.–3:00 p.m.	
3:00 p.m.–4:00 p.m.	
4:00 p.m.–5:00 p.m.	
5:00 p.m.–6:00 p.m.	
6:00 p.m.–7:00 p.m.	
7:00 p.m.–8:00 p.m.	
8:00 p.m.–9:00 p.m.	
9:00 p.m.–10:00 p.m.	
10:00 p.m.–11:00 p.m.	
11:00 p.m.–12:00 a.m.	

2. *Of your responsibilities, which do you not value? Why are they in your schedule?*

Responsibility You Don't Value	Why is it in Your Schedule?

3. Write down your priorities. Even if you
don't make time for them, what are they?
What do you wish you had time to do?

4. Do these priorities appear on your schedule? Which ones do, and which ones don't?
How do you fit in time for those that do?

5. Go back to your schedule and cross out what you wish did not exist. Cross out what you don't value from that schedule.

6. Replace those blocks with your priorities.

7. Create your free block.

8. Fill in the gaps with your leisure activity of choice.

SOCIAL MEDIA AND THE BUSY BRAG CARD

Social media pushes this lifestyle while also showcasing movements of the self-care variety…. yet both directions are distorted.

Direction 1: Look how busy I am! Look how much work I have! Look at me running around! I have no free time! I'm always working! I'm doing everything at once! I have no time for what I care about! I'm so miserable!

Direction 2: Make time for yourself. Take care of yourself. Make time for self-care.

Direction 1 is flawed for reasons previously discussed. No brag card comes attached to overworking yourself, to convincing yourself you are too busy to function. No brag card is attached to depriving yourself of the **human ability** to make time for what you care about. We can all make time for what we care about. We don't have any valid excuses.

Direction 2 is flawed for the misunderstanding that self-care is a separate entity from work; self-care, rather, must be *engraved within our work lives*. It is not a *separate practice*. Self-care is *how* we approach our work…. Self-care is not setting aside time for a face mask or making time to be with friends. Rather, self-care is *embedded* in HOW we work; self-care is our habits. **Self-care is *how we treat ourselves every second of every day*.**

Self-care is approaching a job in such a way to *not* be miserable, but rather enjoying working toward our craft in a way that enables us to instill a passion in our everyday practices.

Self-care is taking care of ourselves *every hour and every second of each day. It is not a separate entity.*

In order to *incorporate* self-care into every hour and every second of your day, you must ask yourself,

"Will completing this action help or hurt my mental health?"
"Will completing this action better me in any way?"
"Will completing this action put me ahead or behind?"
Then, make your decision.

> *Self-care is taking care of ourselves every hour and every second of each day. It is not a separate entity.*

YOU ARE NOT TOO BUSY

> *We can all make time for what we care about. We don't have any valid excuses.*

Running around with little time for what you actually care about is a flawed way of living.
Flooding your schedule at an unhealthy rate is a flawed way of living.
Not having time for quality leisure is a flawed way of living.

I had no time to do anything I cared about.

UNTIL I REALIZED EVERYTHING IS A CHOICE.
I finally understood that lifestyle was being forced upon me. I was being heavily influenced. I was being influenced by how those around me directed their lives, and I was summoning that same demon—the demon of stress, frenzy, and chaos— into my life. I felt I was too busy because everyone around me was too busy. I didn't have time for what I cared about because no one around me had time for what I cared about. If I did have time, I was doing something wrong. I wasn't working hard enough. I wasn't being the best student I could be. I was behind.

Whether you make time for those around you or let your schedule consume you is your choice. You have the choice to declutter your life or to let societal standards make you feel you have to be everywhere all the time.

GUILT AND LEISURE

Joined by my newfound busy brag card, as a college student, I am predisposed to feelings of *guilt* that stem from *merely letting myself be,* a guilt that stems from letting myself relax.

"I didn't get anything done today, I'm so unproductive."
"I was so lazy today."
"Ugh, I sat and watched Netflix all day."
"I need to get some work done."

Students feel guilty for not working hard enough. Students feel guilty for having a day to simply be. Students feel guilty for not working towards their academics in one way or another.

"We must replace the toxic view of resting as sloth or laziness with the understanding that when we celebrate rest for ourselves and others, we make the world safer for everyone"
—AMELIA NAGOSKI, DMA AND AUTHOR

Doing something you don't *want* to do but rather *need* to do does not equate to productivity.

Overworking yourself does not equate to productivity.

Avoiding leisure does not equate to productivity.

Are you truly proud of running out of your eight-hour shift to the grocery store, then darting to the library to study before finally getting some rest? **Are we truly going to idolize that?** Long work days, frantically getting from A to B to C, devoting less and less time to family, friends, sleep, exercise, and more and more time to traffic and frustration? Do we truly want that from our lives? **There has to be more to life.**

And there is more.

We must value rest. We must value leisure. We must value free time. It is in our control. We must take control of this lifestyle we have enslaved ourselves to.

> *We must take control of this lifestyle we have enslaved ourselves to.*

Making time for things you love is productive. Making time for your hobbies is productive. Sleeping in on Sunday is productive. You are making time for what you value. That is more productive than anything else.

> We must make time for what we value above all else.

DISCOVERING YOUR EXTERNAL LIGHT

—

I started to play piano when I was seven years old. I'd always had a love for instruments and music, so my mom signed me up for weekly lessons. Every Wednesday afternoon was my favorite time of the week; I could go make cool sounds from a mega instrument, as I'd call it. In the beginning, I was only completing exercises and short segments of songs, so nothing complete. In time, I learned my first full song, and I was stoked. "Twinkle Twinkle Little Star" became my everything. I played it on my bedroom keyboard for hours on end, and even threw concerts for my parents on several occasions. Luckily for them, I played on a keyboard, not a grand piano stationed in the middle of the house, so I didn't make their ears bleed entirely.

But as I got older and lessons became more intense, practice became more of a chore than a delight or something I looked forward to. I began to loathe those same Wednesday afternoons and begged my mom to cancel my lessons. I would complain for days on end about how hard they were getting and how small my teacher made me feel. The pieces I learned felt forced, none of them were anything I enjoyed learning or performing. I even once recorded the entire lesson to play back later to my mom and prove how mean she was. Oh man, the mind of an eleven-year-old. Eventually, I stopped lessons and began to learn on my own. Then, my love for the piano absolutely skyrocketed. I would look up YouTube tutorials and use the skills I had learned from my years of lessons to learn new songs quickly and personalize every piece. Eventually, I moved on from YouTube tutorials and shifted to learning by ear. I was able to hear songs or find their corresponding chords and play the song with my own taste. The opportunities were endless. I found myself constantly sitting at the piano, losing track of time. I never loathed it, I never tried to avoid it. I would wake up in the morning and run to the piano, the one stationed in the middle of the house, and play away. I was able to play what I wanted with my personal touch. Again: sorry, Mom and Dad.

Coming to college, I was sure I'd lose the one form of leisure that had brought me so much joy. I began to subconsciously fulfill the prophecy of a college student: an absurdly-tight schedule that left little room for my health and wellbeing, and, of course throwing away every hobby that was once important to me.

I wasn't sure I would have time to play, or if I would be able to access any instruments to use at all. I would no longer have a keyboard just a foot away from my bed, nor would I have the time to play like I had when living at home. But I was wrong. Yes, college is busy. But you *can* make time for the things you truly care about. If you have time to scroll through Instagram or get distracted, you have time to do something that is worth your time, whether it be for ten minutes or an hour.

Playing piano is my therapy. It calms me down. It makes me lose sight of everything hectic or out of my control and drills my mind into music. I am able to translate my emotions, feelings, and ideas onto black and white keys. I am able to make something of myself. And I do exactly that, every single day. Every day, at some point in between classes, I run to the Schoenberg Music Building. I take a peek in each classroom, find an empty one, and run to the beautiful grand Yamaha awaiting me in the front. I log out of the real world and enter my musical fantasy. I am relieved of all stressors and distractions and thrown into my paradise. I make time every day for this because coming to understand the value of self-care and mental health protection has turned my life around. Making time for what makes you happy is foundational for any success. We sometimes fall victim to the belief that success gives happiness, but it's the other way around. Happiness grants success. Happiness grants productivity. Happiness aligns you with what is truly important: taking care of yourself and devoting time to academics. Once I started to make time every single day to do this one thing that makes me happy, my stress was relieved. I have become the happiest I have ever been and am now more productive as well. I no longer struggle to get out of bed in the morning and am excited to take on each day. I have deepened my understanding of my purpose. I encourage you to find one thing that makes you ecstatic and make time for it every single day. Whether it be taking a walk on a certain trail or reading a chapter of your favorite book, make time for it and be consistent. Use discipline to build a habit that will be impossible to break. Your health and emotional stability are what will guide you to everything you want to achieve. They come first. So, find your piano.

Find something that gets you going, that gets you excited. It could be anything. Where should you start?

You have to be willing to play the game, one which will throw you into trial after trial, and win. You have to be willing to try. Explore different activities, work to perfect that activity, and watch passion follow shortly after. You have now found your form of leisure.

Make a promise to yourself to discover your external light. What will you explore? What interests you? What seems even in the slightest interesting to you?

1.

2.

3.

4.

5.

THE POWER OF DELIBERATE PRACTICE

———

But what could possibly fill the gap in our lives meant for leisure? What if we have no craft we are interested in pursuing, what if we feel we have no passion? What if we have no hobby we want to perfect or pursue?

No one was born with the ability to do as they do. Frederick Chopin was not born with the ability to play the piano as he did. Michael Phelps was not born with the ability to swim four hundred-meter laps in three minutes and twenty-seven seconds. Kobe Bryant was not born with the ability to shoot game-winners in the clutch on a constant basis. Serena Williams was not born with the ability to hit serves that opponents could never return. No college professor was born with the knowledge they have. Everyone has taken a journey, despite how hidden some may seem. Everyone has had practice.

Each of them had a beginning. **No one starts at the finish line.** The time has come to acknowledge the beauty of beginnings and believe in the process of improvement. We cannot compare our first year of training to someone else's seventh. You wouldn't compare your scrambled eggs to those of famous chef Gordon Ramsay's, right? So enough with this constant comparison and enough with this neglect of the rough patches every single person goes through while trying to reach the next level.

Everyone starts somewhere. *Everyone.* **We all start somewhere.**

I am bringing back Cal Newport, since his work connects largely to the concepts I'm discussing here. In an interview with Tom Bilyeu about Newport's book, *So Good They Can't Ignore You,* Newport explains how the defining factor in someone's successes can be easily chalked up to **deliberate practice.** He recalls some research he did when writing the work, where he questioned the defining characteristics between a mediocre guitar player and a *great* guitar player, for example: "He was so intense when he was practicing the guitar that he would forget to breathe ... and the whole difference is [the mediocre player] never did that."[23]

If you want to get really good at *anything*, Newport explains, you need to tell yourself, "What I need to do is be better at this.... and so I'm gonna push myself beyond where I'm comfortable."

---

23 "(5) How to Quit Social Media and Master Your Focus | Cal Newport on Impact Theory—YouTube." https://www.youtube.com/watch?v=ROKQHRfh2mA.

SEEK DISCOMFORT IN YOUR DELIBERATE PRACTICE. THAT IS THE ONLY WAY YOU WILL SEE RESULTS.

"Deliberate practice stretches you.... just like a muscle. You have to tire out the muscle, exhaust it if you want to experience growth.... and it will be very uncomfortable ... and that's why people don't do it," Newport explains.

Take control and find three potential hobbies you can bring to life, hobbies you will deliberately practice and can reach mastery in. Heighten your external light. You do not need to have a certain passion for that activity just yet, but rather you have to be dedicated enough to *perfect a skill you have not yet perfected.* It's not about passion. **It's about skill,** and once the skill is deliberately practiced, the passion naturally forms; let your practice guide you. Overcome the learning curve and then assess, *"Am I enjoying this?"*

In *So Good They Can't Ignore You,* he debunks the common idea that passion drives career success, and how instead, skill does. Because once we are skilled at some activity, we begin to enjoy it more, and we begin to form a passion for it. **Passion is the result, not the initial driving force.** So, do not be held back because you feel you don't have anything you are passionate about; first find something that relatively interests you. Perfect that skill. Watch your passion form shortly after....

Now, return to the list you made from the last section. Pick one and deliberately practice towards unlocking that external light.

DISCOVERING YOUR EXTERNAL LIGHT: PRACTICE CARD

WHAT

What do you want to work towards? What external light would you like to unlock and perfect? What do you want to get better at or learn more about?

WHY

Why does this interest you? What are your underlying motivations?

HOW

How are you going to explore your *what*? Are you going to read multiple books on a certain topic, listen to podcasts, watch YouTube videos or sign up for class? *How* are you going to get there?

WHEN

Most importantly, *how often* and *when* are you going to devote time to it? Brainstorm a strict schedule below.

CHECK INS & ADJUSTMENTS

How are your newly formed boundaries serving you? What is working and what isn't? How do you feel? What adjustments can you make? Do you feel more liberated? Evaluate. Edit your story as much as you want. After all, this story is yours.

THE FLOW STATE

———

The Flow State is the mental state where you are centered, where you have found your peace, where you are unstoppable and have mastered yourself along with your environment. The Flow State is a state of strength and resilience; *you are in flow*. **You are in control**. You have acquired a sense of self and peace, and you are determined to remain in that state, and, more importantly, protect it at all costs. The Flow State includes an understanding for where *control does not exist*, and the power of **releasing** your desire to strategize where *strategy is not welcomed*. The Flow State is a state of freedom, a state of pure joy and excitement for life, a state that every exercise this book has been leading up to. The Flow State is your power.

DISCOVERING YOUR FLOW STATE

No formula exists for discovering your flow state. Your flow state is an understanding of *what* makes you feel empowered, strong, fearless, and joyous, and maximizing *exactly what brings those feelings into your life*, and limiting what detracts. When you are in your flow state, you feel powerful, strong, happy, excited, motivated, grateful, fearless, yourself.... You are in tune with yourself and your desires.

Flip back through this book and begin to extract what you have discovered *makes you feel at peace*, what brings you to your *flow state*. Simply, *what makes you feel great*, and are all of those things *maximized* in your life? Are your priorities *actually being prioritized*?

Are they in full abundance? Once they are, once your energy and attention are completely focused on *what you value*, are you able to feel at peace with yourself?

For example, *When I am in my flow state...*

1. I sleep eight hours every single night.
2. I give gratitude, out loud, every single morning.
3. I read myself to sleep every single night.
4. I tell the people I love that I love them.
5. I tell the people I miss that I miss them.
6. I have a diet filled with vegetables, fruits, lean meat, and as few starchy foods as possible.
7. I incorporate some sort of movement into my routine every single day.
8. I make time for at least thirty minutes of creativity every single day, through reading, writing, or making a playlist.
9. I prioritize time with my family even when I may feel overloaded with work.
10. I see my education as a privilege.
11. I make time to speak on the phone with my friends.
12. I strictly limit time on social media sites.

How would you describe your flow state? What makes you feel grounded, centered, empowered, and at peace? Who adds to your flow? Who detracts? What activities, music, or habits *support* your flow? Write every piece down. Let your flow state be a place where you can return in times of distress, confusion, and worry. Let your flow state guide you when you feel lost. Let your flow state be a constant reminder of the inner peace you are completely capable of feeling. More importantly, *how do you feel when you are in flow?*

My flow state is a state of mind that makes me feel …

When I am in my flow state …

What is your secret recipe? What ingredients do you need to create your ultimate flow state?

DEVIATE AND RETURN

―――

Our story is not meant to be written in one stage. Our story is meant to be tampered with; it is supposed to be edited, dissected, played with, and rewritten. Our story is ours; you are the author of your life. Because when writing a story, the process is quite informal. The final product takes hours upon hours to finally reach; it is not achieved in one setting. It is not achieved in one attempt. A story is a journey that requires intensive thinking, rounds of editing, countless questioning, and changes upon changes to be made. The final product is a product of *change*. No book, in all of history, did not follow a similar process when it was being written.

Your life is no different. You are not supposed to feel in control, stable, or at peace with yourself at all times. You are supposed to feel lost at times. You are supposed to question your decisions. You are supposed to sit in confusion and question your entire being. You are supposed to feel you aren't doing the right thing. You are meant to overthink. You are meant to feel out of touch… This is all normal. This is all part of the journey we call *life*.

However, our job is to *remain in tune with ourselves* during this journey *and welcome these moments of deviation.* We must *welcome these waves,* for they are going to appear regardless of *how hard we try to avoid them.* In times when we lose control, in times when we can no longer strategize, we must rise and allow ourselves to *ride the wave.* We cannot expend extra energy on situations where energy is not welcomed. We must rise.

We must be attentive to our needs, our desires, what we are missing, and what we may have overdone. We must be attentive to ourselves just as a doctor is to his patient. We must *ride these waves even when we have fallen,* yet be willing to get back up.

We will deviate, but our job is to return to our center. Our job is to be dedicated enough to return to our flow state.

You are the author of your life; that is your authority. Your authority rests in your ability to *write,* to *rewrite,* to *delete,* to *edit,* and most importantly, to **share**.... *to control your story as you wish to.* You are the author. This story is yours. Free yourself from the rigid belief in timelines, in rulebooks which you must abide with. Free yourself from any *plan* you have forced yourself to stick to. Allow yourself to edit. Allow yourself to hit delete. Allow yourself to fluctuate. Allow yourself to *change.* For without change, stability cannot be met; deviation must occur if any sort of stability is to be found and maintained.

In times of worry or distress, re-center yourself through your breath, through your ability to attend to your own needs.

Guide yourself as you would guide a friend in need and assure yourself *you will return to your center.* It might not be in this very moment, but *you will return.*

Your job is to protect your flow state, your stability, and peace, at all costs. Your peace is your treasure. Every decision you make must be made with regard to holding onto your peace.

The noise of the outside world will always remain. Storms will always exist, the wind may blow faster on some days than others; these disturbances are unpredictable. Your job is to hold onto your center, to remain stable, despite these disturbances. Think of a tree; despite its surroundings during a storm, the tree may move around, but it remains inside the ground. The tree tries as hard as it can to remain stable. You must do the same.

Most importantly, believe in yourself, and believe in the process. Live your life surrounded by what brings you joy. Saturate yourself with gratitude, love, honesty, vulnerability, fearlessness, authenticity, curiosity, excitement, discomfort, and the unknown. Let yourself explore. Let yourself reach the extraordinary.

Hold onto your center, but welcome deviation. We can't always stay in drive. It's okay to shift gears.

—NICOLETTE KHALIFIAN

THANK YOU & ACKNOWLEDGEMENTS

——

Thank you for picking up this book, for believing in me, and for letting me share what I have been carefully crafting over the past year. Thank you for the support, the love, and the guidance during this journey. As I wrap up this book, I am stunned it has even been written. I am stunned this is real life. I am filled with gratitude and love for everything that has come my way and everything that has led to this project—which has taught me more than I ever thought possible. Thank you.

Thank you to Eric Koester, who decided to reach out to me and ask if I wanted to take on a project like this, for tuning in every week with incredible workshops and guidance. Thank you for believing in me and fellow UCLA creators. Thank you for dedicating your time and energy to changing the lives of *millions* through your work.

Thank you to Brian Bies, Head of Publishing at New Degree Press, for believing in every single one of us, for pushing us all to the finish line despite our doubts and fears. Thank you for readily making the time to individually guide us, share your knowledge, and push us harder and harder. Thank you for everything.

Thank you to the entire team at New Degree Press for all the hard work and dedication you all show to your authors. Thank you for believing in the youth, for giving us a platform to be heard. Without you, young authors would not exist to the extent they now do.... Thank you.

Thank you to my parents. Mom and Dad ... without your support and your strong-willed push for your children to pursue education and their passions, I wouldn't have ever thought it was possible to publish my work.

Thank you to my brothers, Nathan and Jaden, for the constant stream of *unspoken love* I have been able to somehow translate to myself. Thank you for inspiring me each and every day to be better, to do better, and mostly, to love as hard as I possibly can.

Thank you to my dear friends and family who have both purchased and preordered copies, for allowing me to share my voice to people beyond my immediate reach. Thank you for making *Control Mindset* greater than I ever imagined.

I dedicate this book to anyone who has ever felt lost, silenced, or stuck, for I have been there, *we have all been there.* Your state of being is temporary, and you are entirely capable of living a life you deserve to live. We all are. Every single one of us. Thank you for taking this journey with me.

Made in the USA
San Bernardino, CA
26 June 2020